THE CHEEKY GUIDE TO BRIGHTON

SIXTH EDITION

**Written and researched by
David Bramwell
and Tim Bick**

*Additional material by
Laura Bird*

The Cheeky Guide to Brighton 6th edition

Created by David Bramwell and Tim Bick
Comments/idle tittle-tattle: david@cheekyguides.com
Offers of cash/compliments on new hairstyle: tim@cheekyguides.com
ISBN 9780956130327
Published in 2015 by Cheekyguides Ltd
Europa House, Goldstone Villas, Brighton BN3 3RQ
www.cheekyguides.com

Thanks to the following contributors:

Duncan Hall for In Defence Of Hove (pp 34-35), Fred Pipes for Open Houses
(p42) and Weird Cycle Lanes (p239); Marcus O'Dair for braving those cold
Brighton waves which can tower over 10cm high in Surfing in Brighton (p57);
Phil Lucas for Where To Sit On Brighton Beach (pp82-83), Paul Abbott for map
(pp82-83); Doug Devaney for Percolations (p96-97); Joseph Nixon for Vegetarian
Brighton (p101); Anna and Craig for Northerners Down South (pp104-105);
Jonny Young for Harvey's Beer (p138); Nick Pynn for My Brighton p159.
Special thanks to Heather Dowling, Anna Moulson for The Music Scene, and Amy
Burchill for Veggie Food.

Photo credits

Matt Preston: Phoebe's grave, pebbles, Jane Bom-Bane pp5, 8, 107; Alexis
Maryon: naked boys p13; Peter Chrisp: snowman p32; Barry McFarlane:
Volks Railway p39; Brighton Swimming Club: pp56, 57; Unknown photographer
(every effort has been made to trace them): BOAT p152; Fred Pipes: Disco Pete
p166; Clive Andrews: birdlady p170; Eve Poland: Dolly Rocket p171;
Eric Paige: Storm men p183; Toby Amies (tobyamies.com): fairy p184.

Illustrations

Huge thank yous as always to Lisa Holdcroft for the cover and innumerable
cartoons that appear in this book. She can be contacted at lisaholdcroft.com/
(01273) 705658.

Editing

Sadie Mayne

Cheeky Profile #1: MR TIM BICK

Despite spending 85% of his time naked and being a long-standing Brighton resident, Tim has never visited Bristol Gardens Naturist Health Spa. He says this is because "their sandwiches aren't that good." A typical Piscean, Tim does imitations of orchestral brass instruments, collects exotic fruit, and has an irrational fear of fish and chips.

Lives in: Brighton's fashionable 'Muesli Belt' better known as Hanover
Best feature: inner ear
Favourite metal: tungsten
Cheeky fact: during the research for this book Tim heard about a new seafront club that had just opened that day. He rushed down there within minutes but it had already gone out of business.
Not many people know that: Tim's tongue is so long, he could wear it as a large scarf in winter, though he chooses not to.
Most likely to say: 'That was already damp when I sat down.'

Cheeky Profile #2: DR DAVID BRAMWELL

Having lived in Brighton for over twenty years now David still recalls those halcyon days when the beach was sandy, traffic wardens helped you double park and only sailors had tattoos. A typical Aries, he enjoys shouting, wrestling woodland creatures and going 'brrrr'.

Lives in: Brighton's unfashionable district of disgruntled teachers; better known as Hanover.
Best feature: coccyx
Favourite metal: zinc
Cheeky fact: during research for this book David accidentally took magic mushrooms and scaled the i360. He returned with a pocket full of screws but they're probably not important.
Not many people know that: David makes sculptures of the royal family out of courgettes.
Most likely to say: 'I do apologise, I had cabbage for lunch.'

CONTENTS

In the beginning there was only herring...

1500s Brighton starts life as a prosperous fishing village, paying the government 400 herring a year in taxes.

1783 The town becomes a fashionable health resort when the noted Dr Russell declares that drinking seawater will get rid of boils and put hairs on your chest. Not advisable today unless you want to get rid of your hair and sprout boils on your chest instead.

1790s Brighton's first massage parlour is opened by self-styled "*Shampooing surgeon to His Majesty, King George IV*" Sake Dean Mahomed. It is in actual fact, a **genuine** massage parlour, unlike the ones advertised in the back of *Friday Ad*, but that doesn't stop a flood of missives from lonely gentlemen seeking 'relief'.

1823 The Prince Regent has the Royal Pavilion built as somewhere he can bring back a few mates after the pubs have closed.

1938 Movie star Johnny Weismuller opens the brand-new lido at Saltdean with the immortal line "*Me Tarzan, you Saltdean Lido*".

1940 The West Pier is chopped in half by the War Office to prevent (and we quote) "*a German invasion via the ice-cream kiosk*".

1960s Brighton is host to the 1964 *It's a Knockout*, featuring Mods and Rockers battling it out on the seafront. The town remains a popular choice for deckchair rage for the next twenty years.

1972 Sir Laurence Olivier campaigns fiercely for kippers to be returned to the menu on the Brighton Belle railway line. He succeeds (for a while).

1974 The Eurovision Song Contest is held at the Dome Theatre. Swedish supergroup Abba scoop this prestigious award with *Waterloo*, while neighbouring Norway again scored "*nul points*" with *Yes, We Have No Roll-Mop Herring*.

1979 *Quadrophenia* is released and Sting has his equity card revoked. Scuffles start up again on the beach for a while as the Mods completely miss the point of the movie.

1984 Lady Thatcher visits the bathroom and survives the IRA bombing of the Grand Hotel. Others are not so lucky.

1995 The West Pier is declared an independent state by a bunch of squatters but after two weeks they run out of Rizlas and abandon their plans.

2001 Brighton achieves city status after 1,000 cyclists ride all the way to Downing Street to present Mr Blair with several compromising photographs of him and the entire cast of The Ladyboys of Bangkok, taken during the Labour Conference here in 1992.

2002 A quarter of a million people turn up for a mass piss-up on the beach. The Fatboy Slim gig isn't bad either.

2003 The West Pier burns down and 20,000 starlings are made homeless.

2010 Caroline Lucas becomes the UK's first Green MP.

2013 Local prankster Chris Parkinson puts a spoof ad for a flatmate on Gumtree offering free rent for anyone 'willing to dress up as a walrus'. This goes viral and is seen by film director Kevin Smith who buys the rights to the story and releases the film *Tusk* the following year.

2014 A sinkhole appears on Brighton seafront's main road. The council puts some cones around it and hopes it'll go away.

2015 Brighton's new terrestrial channel, Latest TV, is in full swing, boasting such programmes as: *I'm a Tattooed Vegan Rockabilly, Get Me Out of Here, Educating Portslade*, and *My Big Fat Lactose-Intolerant, Shamanic Transgender Wedding*.

2016 The i360 is opened on Brighton seafront. Views from the top are spectacular, largely owing to the fact that it's the only place in Brighton from which you can't see the i360.

2020 Brighton's last remaining untattooed resident, undertaker Colin Plank, crumbles under intense peer pressure and has 'Dead? Cool.' inked on his neck.

BRIGHTHELMSTONES

Legend has it that a stone circle once stood in the Old Steine but was smashed up by farmers in the early 1800s and eventually used to form the base of Victoria Fountain. Interesting to note that steine means 'stone' in Old English, and the stones in the fountain are sarsen, the same ones used for Stonehenge.

PHOEBE HESSEL

Phoebe Hessel, a trader of fish, pincushions, gingerbread and apples, was a local celebrity in Brighton during the late eighteenth and early nineteenth centuries, and lived through six different monarchies to the glorious old age of 108. She was a celebrity, however, not for her longevity and comestibles but thanks to her heroism and love. The story goes that when her lover, Samuel Golding, prepared to leave Brighton and join the army, Phoebe was unwilling to desert his side and so accompanied him disguised as a man. The two served in the army for 17 years and even fought and were wounded at the Battle of Fontenoy!

OK, so the fact that Phoebe lived to a ripe old age certainly gave her plenty of time to embellish her tale, and we are inclined to wonder how she hid her boobs for all those years, but the story has a happy ending, as the pair finally returned and got married.

Her grave can be found in the churchyard of St Nicholas halfway up Dyke Road, where it is surrounded by a small metal fence to keep out dwarves.

THOSE PEBBLES

Possibly one of the most curious (and certainly most persistent) Brighton myths centres around the origin of the pebbles on our beaches. Some of the most sensible Clarks-shoes-wearing friends still swear blind that all the stones were deposited here in the 20s to prevent beach erosion and that Brighton actually once had sandy beaches. Where this story originated is a mystery but it does throw up a few interesting questions for the believers of this myth, such as: where are the photos and newspaper stories about such a mammoth undertaking? Where were the stones from? And don't the stones run for more than 100 miles of coast? What kind of loony would pebbledash 100 miles of glorious sandy beaches? And besides, what's a groyne for anyway?

MURDER MYSTERY

Take one of the tours during the festival and you will learn about some of the gruesome murders that happened in the 20s and 30s here. There are many accounts of body parts deposited around town in trunks, and a bagged, severed head is said to have been left in the old Horse and Groom bar in Hanover.

One year a friend, Jason, decided to do the murder tour and left his house to walk down to Bartholomew Square where it was starting. The guide introduced the tour by saying:

"We'll commence by visiting the location of probably the most gruesome murder Brighton has ever known," and proceeded to walk the group back to Margaret Street.

"Hey this is the street where I live!" he thought, with growing alarm.

"And it was in this house that the body was dismembered and stored in a cupboard for two weeks..." said the guide, pointing at Jason's bedroom window.

Jason now lives in America.

SUBTERRANEA

Perhaps it's down to childhoods filled with Blyton-esque stories of bookcases that swivel open to reveal secret staircases disappearing darkly down, but virtually every long-term Brighton resident has a tale of some underground tunnel or other. Some of the most popular stories are of a vast network of tunnels emanating from the Pavilion, used by Prinny (the Prince Regent) for everything from visiting Mrs Fitzherbert's pad on the Old Steine, to puffing on a pipe in a Western Road opium den, to riding his horse back and forth from the stables across the road. That aside, there really *is* a tunnel under the Pavilion gardens, built during the Prince's latter-day publicity-shy era, to get him to his stables (now the Dome) without being spotted by the paparazzi.

PATCHAM MAN

If you've ever driven out of Brighton past Preston Park up to the roundabout you will undoubtedly have noticed a strange creature standing by the bus stop in Patcham village, sometimes dressed in a fluorescent jacket, sometimes in a floor rug, perhaps sporting a hubcap for a head or maybe a watering can. It's been there for donkey's years now but it's still a mystery as to who created it. Whoever they are they're ruddy persistent - bits of the poor thing are regularly half inched, but endlessly replaced, producing a constantly morphing sculpture. Or is it simply evolving like any other lifeform? Some locals will try and tell you it was put there to slow motorists down, by making them think it's a small policeman. Others claim it is yet more evidence that voodoo is being practised in the nether-regions of the city which, knowing Brighton, is is more likely.

Pre-op Patcham Man

BRIGHTON PEERS
by Cool CHEESE

DAY TRIPPER

LIVES: CROYDON

SPOTTED: PARADING UP AND DOWN THE SEAFRONT. IN ALL THE AMUSEMENT ARCADES

BEETROOT SUNTAN AND FLUORESCENT EYEBROWS

WRAPAROUND SHADES THAT COST TWO POUNDS FROM A STALL BY THE WEST PIER

PINT OF LAGER IN A PLASTIC GLASS FROM THE FORTUNE OF WAR

TOP OFF AND TUCKED INTO WAISTBAND OF JEANS

TORSO MORE OF A BEER BARREL THAN A SIX-PACK

GIRLFRIEND STAGGERING ALONG BEHIND WITH GIANT TOY HE'S WON ON THE PIER

Here, There and Everywhere

MUSSELS COCKLES WHELKS

KEMPTOWN

Cross over the Old Steine from the bottom of North Street and you'll find yourself in Kemptown, a haven of B&Bs, cafés, restaurants, naughty shops and home to much of Brighton's gay and lesbian community, not to mention its eccentrics. Here you're likely to buy your strawberries next to a drag queen in Morrison's or witness (as we have) two guys rolling around on the street half-naked at three in the morning singing "the hills are alive with the sound of music". Kemptown may not be a part of Brighton that has been dressed up for visitors, but it is the rough edges that actually provide much of the appeal. Perhaps in truth this is the part of Brighton that truly deserves the label 'bohemian'. After all, where else in the world would a local charity shop (the Sussex Beacon) have had an annual sale of second-hand rubberwear and bondage gear?

To explore Kemptown take a walk up St James's Street and keep going: you'll find great cafés like Neighbourhood and Red Roaster, health food stores, barbers, gay-lifestyle boutiques and innumerable bars. Venture down the side streets that run to the sea from St James's Street and you'll soon discover where the bulk of Brighton's B&Bs and hotels are to be found.

As you're walking up St James's Street from the Old Steine, take the time to seek out George Street on your left. Here you'll find two of the town's most flamboyant eateries, Bom-Bane's and the Tea Cosy, as well as the Queen's Arms offering drag queen karaoke seven days a week. And keep your eyes peeled for the twitten just after the Tea Cosy. Last time we visited it had its own 'Fridge Library'.

Continue further up St James's Street, past the Sidewinder, cyclops crab painting and Hand in Hand, where it becomes St George's Road. Here Kemptown begins to feel more like a village. No surprise that it is actually known as Kemptown Village. Nowhere in Brighton will you find a more pleasant, active and friendly community. Recommended eateries include the coffee shop Ground, Compass Point (for American-inspired cuisine) and the Barley Mow pub,

which comes with its own tuckshop. There's a wealth of good shops here including Vintage Workshop, Kemptown Bookshop and Pardon My French.

Continue on, past the old mausoleum that is now Proud Cabaret Brighton, and eventually you'll reach Sussex Square and Lewes Crescent. These stunning white flats are occupied by some of Brighton's most affluent bohemians, and have housed their fair share of celebrities – Lewis Carroll, Cate Blanchett, Gaz Coombs, Kevin Rowland, Nick Cave and Howard Marks, to name but a few. If you want to head back into Brighton you can simply turn on your heels. Alternatively, you could take a stroll back along the seafront, though (depending on your tastes) you may have to turn a blind eye to the furtive men enjoying a bit of rough and tumble in the bushes at Duke's Mound.

A shopper peruses the available wares in Kemptown's red light district

SIX AMAZING NORTH LAINE FACTS

1. North Laine *is* spelled North Laine.

2. With the exception of Bert's Homestore in Kensington Gardens, it's impossible to buy anything of practical use here.

3. The Bonsai Shop in Sydney Street has mysteriously remained open for nearly thirty years despite the fact that no-one has ever seen a customer buying a bonsai, let alone entering the shop.

"We'll come back when they've got some bigger trees in stock."

The Slow Cowboy, at a standstill

4. Anyone caught shop-lifting in North Laine is sentenced to two years hard labour selling bird whistles.

5. The sorting office on North Road has a strict policy of only employing heavily tattooed rockabillies and lesbians.

6. North Laine is owned by an eccentric billionaire known as The Slow Cowboy. Painfully thin and walking as if on broken glass, SC dresses to impress, his wardrobe ranging from dayglo suit and a mohican to looking like he stepped out of *Yellow Submarine*.

NORTH LAINE

www.northlaine.co.uk

Glamorous, young, posey, vibrant and pretentious it may be, but Cleethorpes High Street it is not: this colourful area of Brighton is like Haight Ashbury, Carnaby Street and Greenwich Village, all squeezed into just a handful of streets.

Many of the independent shops here are kitsch, retro or shamelessly glitzy; if it's silver thigh-high platforms, a kimono or a Ganesh ashtray you're after, you'll be spoilt for choice. And while some of the shops' merchandise seems perfectly normal to Brightonians it can appear a tad bizarre to new visitors – Cybercandy's scorpion lollies, Pussy's range of offensive greetings cards and pretty much anything in the Guarana Bar.

Unsurprisingly, North Laine is a posers' paradise. From 80s retro to steampunk, every fashion gets a look-in. Walk down Kensington Gardens in full KISS make-up with cream crackers stuck to you and few heads will turn.

Priding itself on its café culture, North Laine really blossoms during the summer months when balconies heave with frappuccinos and tables and chairs fill the streets. It's a pleasure then just to hang out in some of the cafés here and watch the world and its dog go by, The Dorset and Pavilion Gardens Café being particularly favourable haunts,

While it would be remiss of us not to mention the ongoing gentrification of Brighton – resulting in the arrival of such unwelcome retail titans as Tesco and Starbucks – the truth is, it'd take more than a few trendy eateries and chains to spoil things here. The old adage "in North Laine anything goes" is as pertinent as ever. Don't be surprised if after an afternoon's visit you end up going home with a leopardskin suit, pierced genitals and a live monkey: that's just a typical day's shopping in North Laine.

THE (OLD) LANES

A series of confusing narrow passages and attractive streets make up this area of Brighton, which is steeped in history and tales of smugglers, ghosts and randy nuns. The passages are known locally as twittens, (an old smugglers' term for 'thin street with over-priced jewellery shops') and are enclosed by West Street, North Street, East Street and the seafront. You'll enjoy wandering around here and perusing the shops – but don't worry if you get lost, even long-term residents do from time to time.

At the centre of the maze lies the dolphin sculpture in the fountain at Brighton Square. It is an old Brighton custom to run around it three times, throw your trousers in and make a

wish, though for the more prudish a coin will suffice.

Choose from any number of enticing eateries here, such as Terre à Terre, AguaDulce or English's, but don't leave without sampling a coffee at Marwood, doughnut at the Mock Turtle, or cream tea at Blackbird. And don't forget to poke your head in at Fabrica Gallery on Ship Street to see what latest art installation they have in this beautiful building.

In summer the Old Lanes is also a popular area for street entertainment. On East Street you'll often find jazz bands, performance artists and tarot readers. Once we saw a girl here busking with a rat. She kept it on her shoulder while playing her guitar, and now and again she let it drink from her mouth. Eurgh!

THE SEAFRONT

"The beach washes away the ills of mankind." Dr Richard Russell

Stretching from the nudist beach by the Marina across to Hove and beyond, this is really the key inspiration behind all that is Brighton. In summer it's always swarming with life – families with kids, groups of foreign visitors, young couples engaging in heavy petting and the obligatory weirdo with a metal detector.

When the sun is out you'll doubtless want to join the crowds down here, brave the sea for a swim, kayak, hang around the cafés or just loll around on the beach slowly turning the colour of strawberry jam.

The most popular stretch lies between the two piers. Here you'll find clubs, amusement arcades, the Fishing Museum, the carousel, the Artists' Quarter, palmists and an assortment of outdoor entertainment during summer. If you want a good walk, follow the seafront path all the way to the multi-coloured beach huts in Hove and stop for food at the Meeting Place Café. The area between the piers is also a hotspot for several of Brighton's

clubs – on summer evenings you can expect the clubbing crowd to be out in force, particularly around the Fortune of War, Tempest and other seafront bars.

East of Brighton Pier is Madeira Drive. This area comes alive when there are car and motorbike rallies which, in summer, appear to be every other weekend. The loopiest of these is the coach rally, where identically dressed white-shirted drivers in black ties, replete with

Hey, I found another ring-pull ⓱

Get orf
my larnd!

'steering bellies', demonstrate their skills at parking and slaloming their lurching behemoths between sets of cones.

Madeira Drive has seen some rejuvenation in the last ten years with the excellent Jungle Rumble Adventure Golf and Yellowave beach volleyball, both of which have nifty cafés. Lacking many clubs and bars does mean that in summer the stretches of beach here are mercifully quieter than between the two piers. Running along here all the way to the Marina however, is the miniature Volk's Railway – a reminder of how much smaller people were in the old days.

If you do take a wander east of Brighton Pier, look out for the Flint Grotto with its stone figures staring out to sea, and the strange old house set into the promenade just beyond the Concorde 2. The story goes that before the promenade was built, all the houses along the front were sold and demolished, apart from one belonging to some stubborn old guy, Carl Vincent, who refused to sell up. The council couldn't move him, so they simply built the promenade over his house.

Continue east and you'll eventually find the nudist beach. Once controversial, now it's mainly populated by the gay community and a character known as Windmill Man. We'll leave you to figure out how he got his nickname.

Whichever part of the beach you prefer, when it's a warm night nothing beats finding a quiet spot with some friends, getting some beers and food, and watching the sun go down. If you're still around after all the clubs have cleared, it does eventually get pretty empty, although there's always the odd clubber who's crashed out after too many pills, and a guy still looking for his contact lens.

And, finally, it's time to come clean. Yes, it's true: there is no sand (except at very low tide) only pebbles. According to Dr Malcolm Cornwall at Brighton University, around 100 billion to be precise and not a decent one for skimming (he also reckons it'd take 2,500 years to count them all at the rate of one per second!) But, as a small compensation, when you take your picnic down the beach and the wind whips up, at least you won't be crunching your way through a tuna-and-sand ciabatta.

GREEN SPACES

Let's face it, Brighton is not renowned for its greenery. Down on the seafront, over the decades, the council seem to have done everything in their power to remove all traces of the stuff, while the town centre has little more than a few patches of grass and some flowerbeds outside the Pavilion. But all is not lost. Head inland and Brighton has a modest selection of parks and open spaces to keep even the most ardent picnickers, tree-huggers and frisbee players happy.

Preston Park
On the A23

Brighton's largest park is located a little way down Preston Road about half an hour's walk from the seafront with two cafés in the middle, a manor house with a pet cemetery, walled garden, thirteenth century church and loads of space for big sports games. While a good place for a picnic, the ever-present noise of cars from the main road can sometimes spoil a tranquil afternoon here so it's best to position yourselves further up the hill if it's peace and quiet you're after.

Preston Park also boasts the UKs oldest cycling track but at the time of going to print it was deemed unsafe and closed until further notice. After the demise of the West Pier and Brighton's ice rink for similar reasons, we're not too hopeful for its return.

The Level
Bottom end of Ditchling Road

Despite the best efforts of the self-appointed 'Friends of The Level', who were unlikely fans of the semi-derelict children's playground full of rusty swings, the council went ahead with a multi-million pound revamp in 2014.

A rare sighting of skateboarders below the age of 50

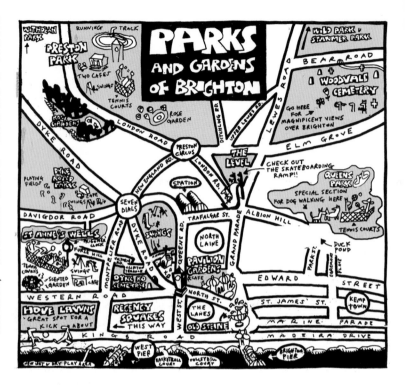

The results are spectacular; what was previously largely a hangout for winos and unconscious post-clubbers is now a vibrant and attractive space stuffed with people having a nice time. Small children run amok in the creatively designed playground, particularly the section where water fountains shoot out of the ground, and larger children (and forty year olds, this is Brighton) mob the sunken concrete skatepark. For the more sedate there's a pétanque, boccia and chess area, and you can even borrow the necessary equipment from the on-site gardener. Or if you'd rather do nothing at all, you can just flop on the grass or chew a flapjack at the newly built Velo Café that sits in the middle of it all.

St Ann's Well Gardens
Somerhill Road, Hove

This small, pretty park in Hove has a scent garden, a family-friendly café, a few picnic areas and tennis courts. It's a popular spot for mums out with the young 'uns and has a resident old lady called Madge, who'll engage you in conversations about boxing given half a chance.

The park's most curious feature has to be the strange clock on a pole that overlooks the tennis courts and bowling green. It's straight out of the 60s cult TV show The Prisoner and, in keeping with the spirit of the programme, never ever tells the right time.

Queen's Park
Between Kemptown and Hanover

Queen's Park may be a bit of a hike if approached from the town centre or seafront, but you'll soon forget those aching corns and bunions once you arrive at this beautifully sculpted park with its sloping hills, large green areas, lake and tennis courts.

If you've come to escape crowds, head around the lake (formerly a rollerskating rink in the 60s) and up the hill to discover such curiosities as the tiny waterfall, the scented garden by the eastern entrance, and the 'wildlife area' full of butterflies, birds and wild fennel in the summer. Such features as this small overgrown wilderness demonstrate that Brighton council can be surprisingly inspired sometimes (though equally it could just be a ploy to save on pruning expenses). Other features to look out for are the park's carved wooden benches and strange old monuments from its former days as part of Thomas Attree's estate.

When you've had enough of the chaos of Brighton in high season, it's good to know there's somewhere you can have a picnic, climb a tree, feed the ducks, play hide and seek in the bushes or simply curl up under an old oak for the afternoon with a good book and a treacle sandwich.

Woodvale Crematorium
Lewes Road/Bear Road

Halfway down the Lewes Road, Woodvale Cemetery is one of Brighton's best-kept secrets. The largest expanse of greenery in the whole of the city centre, it is by turn mysterious, spooky and beautiful, particularly in spring when everything is in bloom.

Wander round its spacious and hilly terrain and you'll stumble across the columbarium, the memorial gardens, odd mausoleums and the little paths that disappear off into the undergrowth. If you want a quest you can look for the graves of Lance Schumacher (one of Custer's men) or the original Mr Hannington, though they might take a good couple of hours to find.

Come on a cold overcast February and it can feel a little sinister, particularly with the hospital high up on Elm Grove towering over like some dark satanic mill. When it's warm, however, the crematorium is the perfect place to clear the cobwebs, draw inspiration, picnic, meditate or simply enjoy a bit of peace in a town that never stops.

The Pavilion Gardens

After a morning's shopping in North Laine, these gardens behind the Pavilion make an ideal spot for a bit of lolling around in the sun. Sure, it gets busy here in summer, with groups of foreign students, picnickers, snogging couples, pigeons and that bloke who's always playing the sax, but it's a pleasant alternative to the concreted seafront and the closest Brighton gets to the cosmopolitan atmosphere of a plaza. It's also one of the rare spots in Brighton with a bit of decent greenery and has a commanding view of the Pavilion to boot.

If you're in need of refreshments the café here offers drinks, hot snacks and those famous rock cakes. Look for the photos on the café history noticeboard on the side of the hut. They sure had big ears in those days.

HOVE...AN APOLOGY?

Dear Readers

Over the years I have offended tens of people by not including Hove in the title of this book, as officially Brighton & Hove has come as a package since 2001. Of course, unless you're a hardcore Hovestrian, you're probably wondering what all the fuss is about. I mean, after all, you say, isn't it just a poor man's Brighton offering accommodation for commuters and old ladies who spend their time making jam and writing angry letters to The Argus? In fact, you shout, rising to your feet in indignation, come on, there are hardly any decent pubs in Hove and the only source of entertainment is watching Zoella walking her pug on Hove Lawns. And while you'd be right in such matters, Hove has got a few tricks up its sleeves, hence we're devoting the rest of this letter to no fewer than ten amazing Hove facts!

Hove fact number one: Hove begins at Boundary Passage (the longest alleyway in Brighton, opposite Little Western Street) and continues all the way to Worthing.
Hove fact number four: Cycling is prohibited on Hove promenade, unless you're riding a penny farthing.
Hove fact number six: Hove has a big Tesco.
Hove fact number seven: Hove is the birthplace of cinema, hip hop, croissants and Jackie Chan.
Hove fact number eight: Hove rhymes with cove.
Hove fact number ten: Hove is very, very close to the magnificent city of Brighton.

Curiously, there is an age-old joke that Hove should be renamed Hove Actually owing to the countless times its residents, when asked if they live in Brighton, reply with snooty indignation – 'No, Hove actually.' As a catchphrase it has become as tiresome as 'Ooh, I could crush a grape' and 'Turned out nice again'. Oh god, now I'm really showing my age. Perhaps I should move to Hove.

Your humble servant
Dr Bramwell
Brighton, obviously

A Superb Modern Block of Flats in a Unique Setting

HOVEDENE

Dear Sir

Re: In Defence of Hove

It has come to my attention that over the last five
editions of your cheeky travel handbook Hove has been
dismissed as an irrelevance to the hip happenings going
on in Brighton.

Apparently Hove is the new Eastbourne, God's waiting
room, the place where people forget why they went there
in the first place.

I am writing to inform you and your tens of readers
that this is far from the case. Hove, or Hove Actually,
is as sick, wicked and hip as anything Skidrow On Sea
can offer, and to prove it I have taken a break from
writing to the editor at The Argus to create one of
those listicles which seem so popular on the interweb
today. Please note I've managed to actually make it ten
reasons rather than your paltry effort.

1 MARROCCO'S ON HOVE SEAFRONT
Forget Mr Whippy, Marrocco's has been making 20-odd
flavours of ice cream since Methuselah was a lad,
ranging from classics like rum and raisin to blue
bubblegum flavour popular among the youngsters. Plus
there's an Italian restaurant at the back something
Hove can never have enough of.

2 CITY BOOOKS AND THE BOOK NOOK
Brighton may have turned to the Kindle, but Hove still
has those big papery things with City Books an honest-
to-goodness book shop which even Amazon couldn't put an
end to. The Book Nook is a kiddie paradise perfect for
improving gifts for the grandkids.

3 HOVE MUSEUM AND ART GALLERY
Whenever you're getting nostalgic for the old days its
worth heading down New Church Road for the exhibitions

of the toys from your childhood and those old films on a loop like they just dont make any more.

4 THE CRICKET GROUND
Its not summer without the sound of leather on willow, or the ear-splitting pop music played whenever anyone in a 20-20 match hits the ball. Plus the Eaton Road ground is our own Wembley Arena, hosting up and coming acts like Cliff Richard and Elton John over the summer.

5 THE OLD MARKET
They try to pretend they're in Brighton, with their groovy Fringe programming and branding, but The Old Market is ours. And the beauty of having so many shows from the Edinburgh Fringe is that they are all quite short so you can get home early for a nice cup of tea.

6 HOVE BEACH
You won't find hordes of clubbers and out-of-towners here. Instead it's possible to find a quiet patch to read the latest Frederick Forsyth or Jeffrey Archer and doze off without being disturbed by ghetto blasters or smelly barbecues.

7 ITALIAN RESTAURANTS
If you like pizza, pasta and meat in tomato sauces you have more choices than you could ever imagine.

8 THE OLD MARKET
They try to pretend they're in Brighton, with their groovy Fringe programming and...hang on, have I done this one already?

9 CELEBRITIES
They all live in Hove with their pedigree dogs now take that, Brighton.

10 REMEMBER TO BUY CATFOOD AND NEW PANTS
Eh? I'm terribly sorry I seem to have lost my train of thought. What on earth was I talking about? Is it time for my tablets yet?

Angry Of Hove (aged 37 and a quarter)
Hova Villas Retirement Home

BRIGHTON EMBARRASSMENT

THE MARINA

On the outer reaches of Brighton seafront lies the Marina – a concrete jungle of factory shops, casinos, an Asda, fake palm trees, a drive-through McDonalds, the world's most hideous multi-storey car park and a really tacky Walk of Fame for such Brighton celebrities as er… Leo Sayer and er… The Argus. The antithesis of Brighton's saucy, seedy, devil-may-care spirit, the Marina resembles some god-awful nautical theme park crossed with Doncaster town centre. The best solution for this place would be for the council to throw its hands in the air, say "Oops" and send in the bulldozers.

THE AQUARIUM TERRACE

When the original Concorde and go-kart track opposite Brighton Pier were demolished, did the council use the opportunity to add a bit of much-needed greenery to the seafront, or install something fun like an open-air pool? No. Instead it built the Aquarium Terrace – a monstrous white elephant with a dozen or more reasonably sized venues and spaces that have bizarrely remained empty for more than fifteen years!! Even the Burger King and amusement arcade have long since gone leaving just the Harvester. Being opposite the 'UKs most visited free tourist attraction' surely this has to be some of the most valuable land in the country. How can it remain derelict for nearly two decades?? Baffling.

WESTERN ROAD & CHURCHILL SQUARE

While no worse than any other city-centre high street for its homogenised chain stores and coffee franchises, it is the weekend crowds and endless stream of kamikaze buses that make Western Road a place which, unless you're in dire need of new pants and socks from M&S, is best avoided.

WEST STREET

With its amusement arcades, tacky nightclubs, themed pubs and burger bars, West Street is inevitably the first port of call for stag and hen parties, drunk teenagers and anyone looking for a punch-up. The police even have a van permanently stationed here at weekends to save the inevitable callouts. Need we say more?

THE SEAFRONT ARCHWAYS

West of the Brighton Pier, the council have now closed many of the stairways leading down to the seafront. Even walking through Brighton's iconic archways is now deemed unsafe with much of this area cordoned off with metal fencing. With councils crippled by Tory budget cuts it's hard to imagine when or how we'll be able to afford to repair this iconic part of the seafront.

ANSTON HOUSE

Sitting opposite Preston Park on the main A23 route into the city, nothing says "welcome to Brighton" like a big derelict 60s office block surrounded by twelve-foot-high security fencing. Until 2007 the building was at least partly shielded by beautiful, mature, officially protected trees, before an unscrupulous developer decided to chop them down, turn the adjacent green wasteland into a bomb site, stick up an ugly metal fence and then lose interest entirely. Still, it's only been empty for 28 years, what's the rush?

GET A REAL TASTE OF AN ENGLISH
BRIGHTON

Lose loads of money at the American-style Casino.

Marvel at the American-style bowling alley!!

See the stunning American-owned Asda and its huge concrete carpark!

Enjoy an American-style in-car meal at our drive-through McDonald's.

HARBOUR TOWN AT THE
MARINA

Brighton's architectural masterpiece

See all the latest American movies at our multiplex cinema. Over 300 screens and no subtitled foreign shit.

Have fun, get your car washed!!!

Baggage FACTORY

Enjoy our factory-outlet shops offering overpriced tat, Dynasty style blouses for the modern lady and knitwear for rugged men.

Take the Hollywood-style Walk Of Fame with such stars as the Coral Brighton & Hove Greyhound Stadium!!

THE EVENING ARGUS

WALK OF FAME   BRIGHTON   WALK OF FAME

Weird & Wonderful Things, To Do

MUSEUMS & LANDMARKS

The Pavilion

Old Steine (01273) 290900
10am-5.15pm October-March
9.30am-5.45pm April-September
Adults £11.50, children £6.20
residents £5.75
brightonmuseums.org.uk/royalpavilion

While the Pavilion does have those awful little rope chains and hordes of American tourists giving "*oohs*" and "*aaahs*" in every room, it cannot be denied that this building is nothing short of astonishing. An Indian palace in a small English seaside town with a stunning and surprising interior modelled on a top-of-the-range oriental brothel, carpets that would shock the most outré Vegas casino and heaps of gold leaf. Surely that's

got to be worth a look? And it is. Not only is the Pavilion Brighton's most famous landmark but the only British royal palace owned by a local council, and the very emblem of the place. Could you really visit Paris and not go up the Eiffel Tower? Dreamed up and partly designed by Prinny in 1823 as a weekend retreat, this stately pleasure dome helped establish Brighton as a fashionable place to be seen. Nearly two hundred years later, the Prince's devotion to art, music, extravagance and philandering seems to have left an indelible impression on the town.

Step inside and be prepared to enter a labyrinth of bamboo, impressive sculptures, fire-breathing dragons and the most outrageous chandeliers in the universe. "*George clearly had a lot of gay friends,*" as a friend of ours wryly commented. "*All designed to delight and unsettle you,*" the audio guide whispers in your ear. It will. And yet, surprisingly, it all works extremely well, despite being the ultimate in 18th century bling. While upstairs is less dazzling than the ground floor's banqueting hall, kitchens, foyer and sitting rooms, it **is** rich with good stories about the extravagances of the 22-stone prince. For example, he was renowned for his love of women and food and had two secret doors installed in the bedroom, one for his midnight rendezvous with Mrs Fitzherbert and the other for a bloke selling seafood in a basket. Some nights, when the prince got too drunk, he'd get them mixed up and end up eating Mrs F's handbag while making love to the seafood guy. And so began Brighton's celebrated gay scene. But we digress. Holiday cottages do not come more exotic than this.

Top tip: come as early as possible

in the morning to avoid the crowds of foreign language students standing around with sketch pads and questionnaires.

St Bartholomew's Church
Ann Street (01273) 620491
Open Mon-Sat 10am-1pm, 2pm-4.30pm
stbartholomewsbrighton.org.uk

Located behind Trafalgar Street and London Road, St Bartholomew's may be off the beaten track but, as the biggest brick church in Europe, is rather difficult *not* to find. Impressive for its size and Italian Gothic design, inside St Bart's is decorated with oil paintings, Italian mosaics and marble archways and could easily have served as the setting for an old Peter Greenaway film.

It's best visited during Brighton Festival in May when it plays host to a series of concerts ranging from Renaissance choral music to piano recitals.

Brighton Pier

The epitome of cheesy seaside fun. Not only Brighton's most popular attraction but the UK's fifth favourite "free" (in the sense that you can walk on it for nothing) tourist spot to boot. Experience life on the ocean waves with the famous Dolphin Derby, see the Isle of Wight from the top of the Helter Skelter (on a clear day), sing Elvis at Horatio's karaoke bar, wolf down some fish and chips, scream your head off on the big dipper, yawn your way through the ghost train, lose your car keys down the gaps in the floorboards, have your palm read by an Australian backpacker called Gypsy Kevin and get absolutely soaking wet on the log flume. Brighton without Brighton Pier would be like Tommy Cooper without the fez.

The West Pier

A tragedy of epic proportions, the West Pier was cock of the town until it was marooned by a storm in the 70s and left to rot like Miss Haversham's wedding cake. Then in late 2002, over the space of a few months it endured a further storm and two suspected arson attacks

which pretty much destroyed everything. And yet! There, like a small beacon of hope, much to everyone's surprise and delight, the little fortune-telling kiosk bravely hung on. Against all odds it survived. Oh how it cheered our hearts to see it waving the flag of courage when all around was desolation and despair. Then, at the end of 2005, it fell off too.

Some (the Cheeky team included) have grown to love this spinach-encrusted birdcage. If nothing else, it serves as a costly reminder to keep a watchful eye on the things we love in this town and never to allow anything else to fall into rack and ruin. With the exception of the marina, of course.

The Flint Grotto

Madeira Drive, halfway between Brighton
Pier and the Concorde 2

For several years fisherman and artist
Rory McCormack has been quietly
creating this curious piece of outsider
art in a fishing enclosure on Brighton
seafront near the Concorde 2. Made
almost entirely from beach stones
it includes a conch shell archway
and seated and standing figures who
stare out to sea. While not quite on
the same level as Howard Finster's
Paradise Gardens, the grotto is still far
more intriguing than the rest of the
seafront's art sculptures, although it is
best viewed with your back to the sea.

If Rory happens to be around when
you visit and takes a liking to you, he
might even offer you a potato from
what has to be Brighton's only beach-
grown potato patch.

Anna's Museum

Upper North Street
(view from street, don't knock on the door)
annasmuseum.org

Incongruously placed in the front
window of a private house next
door to an osteopath's is this private
collection of mostly – there's no
getting round it – dead things,
that belong to a young girl called
Anna. Whether it's shells, bird's
eggs, skeletons or stuffed squirrels,
everything has been meticulously
labelled by its curator (our favourite
is a white mouse wearing a top hat
whose label says 'Ernest Macabre,
stuffed by Anna') as the display has
evolved over a number of years.
Clearly an interesting young lady, Anna
knows exactly why she has acquired
each piece; a plaque-mounted cow
horn is there *"because it smelt nice."*
She is however growing up fast so nip
round and have a look at the museum
before it gets turned into a shrine to
One Direction or Skrillex.

The i360

Just look into the sky from anywhere in town and you'll spot it
www.brightoni360.co.uk

Already nicknamed the iSore, this was still being constructed at the time of going to print so it would be churlish of us to have any opinion of it until its completion. What can be said however is that while countless residents see it as a white elephant for Brighton at the planned £15 per ticket, some of our Twitter followers think it's going to be an architectural masterpiece and a big hit with the tourists. So thank you Terry and Jemima for your enthusiastic tweet about the i360, and on a separate note, we wish you well in your imminent move from Brighton's Regency Square to New Zealand.

Shoreham power station, soon to be a top tourist attraction

Brighton Museum and Art Gallery

Church Street/Royal Pavilion Gardens
(01273) 290900
Tues-Sun 10am-5pm
Admission £5 adults £2.80 kids,
residents free (with evidence of address)
brightonmuseums.org.uk/brighton

Brighton Museum is a place to be cherished: it's modern, spacious, beautifully lit, packed with imaginative displays and has a sweet little café.

On the ground floor much of the space is given over to the town itself, covering its social history from sport, work and religion to leisure and even England's last cork shop. Wander round and you can watch old videos of Brighton, listen to recorded voices, feel the mystery objects (a dead seagull and a 'Prince Albert'), peruse paintings of Sake Dean Mahomed and Dr Russell, and learn all about the mods and rockers. You're not meant to sit on the scooter in the far-left corner,

but it makes for a terrific photo so go on, be a devil. Thankfully they've not shied away from Brighton's historical penchant for dirty weekends either. From the 'lick my melons' calling card of a 90s brothel to club posters, Brighton's unashamed association with hedonism is well documented. In fact so *much* so that, conversely, the town's long history of alternative/unusual medical practices and as a health resort is given scant attention.

Upstairs are the café and the museum's exhibition space. The remains of the second floor are given over to the history of fashion, containing the Prince Regent's enormous breeches and a brilliant section on the human body. Again in keeping with the residents' rampant narcissism, it covers themes of flesh, skin, body modification, spectators and performers.

And finally, if you've haven't visited for decades and need to see a familiar face, beloved Gallet cat Brunel (a giant model of one of the ornamental pair in the cabinet by Art and Design) is still there by the entrance, awaiting a stroke and your donations.

The Booth Museum of Natural History

194 Dyke Road (01273) 292777
Mon-Sat 10am-5pm, Sun 2pm-5pm,
closed Thurs Admission free
brightonmuseums.org.uk/booth

Originally opened as a private museum in 1874 by bird-stuffing enthusiast Mr Booth, this building has blossomed into one of the focal points and main archives of natural history for the Brighton area. As well as providing a home to thousands of creatures, skeletons and strange things in specimen jars, it is a resource centre for local schools. On special days they even do live taxidermy for the public. Should you stumble across any fresh road kill, just "*scoop it up and bring it in*".

On entering the museum the first thing you'll notice is the smell of mothballs and the wonderfully gloomy atmosphere. Towers of stuffed birds line the walls, while in the centre lie two incongruous but beautiful stained-glass windows.

At this point, if you're in a group, we recommend splitting up and going it alone for maximum effect. Walk down the aisles at the side and enter Hitchcock's terrifying world of *The Birds*. Down the centre you'll find the Victorian parlour, discovery lab – a hands-on science area for kids – and, at the back, an impressive array of skeletons.

Look out for the sheep that looks like Daisy from the Woody Allen movie, the charred remnants of a (half-eaten) dodo, the *Harry Potter* owls and the famous 'toad in the hole'. We bet you won't find the warthog's head though.

What you see in the museum is only a small percentage of what's been collected over the years as, owing to lack of space, they're unable to display

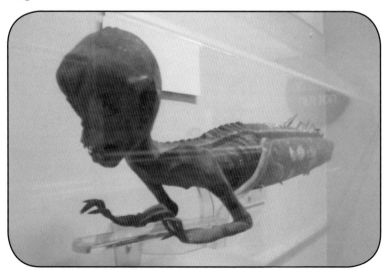

Pom-Pom Birds
Steiff, Germany, 1930s - 1950s
BTMM_DAg_111

Miniature Chick
Schuco, Germany,

everything. With special permission you can get a behind-the-scenes tour. We have been lucky enough to wander through dusty old badger-lined corridors where they've got drawers of flat-packed ducks and a scorpion found by a guest in the Grand Hotel.

To find the museum, follow Dyke Road from the Clock Tower and you'll find it opposite the tennis courts after about a fifteen-minute walk. Could you spend the night here on your own, though? We swear they all come to life then.

Brighton Toy and Model Museum

52/55 Trafalgar Street (01273) 749494
Tues-Fri 10am-5pm, Sat 11am-5pm
Adults £6.50, children/oldies £4
www.brightontoymuseum.co.uk

Housed under a damp railway bridge below Brighton Station, what this museum lacks in setting it makes up for with its pristine collection. There are more than 25,000 exhibits, beautifully displayed and all clearly the pride and joy of founder Chris Littledale.

Model railways make up the bulk of the collection and – unlike their full-scale counterparts upstairs – actually run. In fact, five times a year they go mad and set off *everything* for the day – it's like a scene from *Toy Story 2*. While internationally renowned for the extensive collection of 1930s model trains, there's plenty more to see here, including a toy theatre and puppet section, model cars and Japanese dolls.

Watch out during term time, though: like the Booth Museum you may be surrounded by gangs of kids trying their best to knock over all the little figurines in the cabinets.

Hove Museum

19 New Church Road, Hove
Mon-Sun 10am-5pm, closed Wed
Admission free
brightonmuseums.org.uk/hove

Long gone are the psychedelic carpets and cardboard cut-out of Ringo Starr, but the 1970s teashop still remains (thankfully) in this beautiful old museum in darkest Hove. Downstairs is an exhibition space that changes seasonally, while upstairs the Wizard's Attic and History of Cinema justify the trek here by themselves.

The Wizard's Attic is a room that children (and adults) will thoroughly enjoy. The low-level lighting creates a wonderfully spooky atmosphere (to go with the attic theme); there are toys hanging from the ceiling, little cubbyholes with fairground mirrors, a tin bath full of soldiers, a clock that runs backwards and even a painting where the eyes follow you around the room. And dare you put your hand in the hole below the box full of creepy-crawlies?

Further on, the History of Cinema section tells the history of Hove's (little-known) role as the birthplace of the British film industry. Exhibits range from old zoetropes and magic lanterns to a tiny six-seater cinema showing short films. In *Professor Heard's Magic Lantern Show* a talking skull guides you through a magical journey in which ghosts and goblins rise from a witch's cauldron. Another, *On and Behind the Seafront*, has some classic footage of a bygone Brighton, including the fabulous open-air swimming pool at Black Rock and a troop of elephants wandering down Trafalgar Street and accidentally stepping on someone's cat.

And once you're through horsing around, make sure to pay your respects to Hove's loveable grannies and Mrs Doyle types by popping into the tearooms for a big wedge of cake and a nice hot cuppa.

WEIRD & WONDERFUL THINGS TO DO

Mechanical Memories Museum
Brighton seafront
Open *"when it's nice"*
www.mechanicalmemoriesmuseum.co.uk

Situated between the Palace Pier and the Doughnut, this place opens, closes, opens for a while, closes for good, re-opens under new management, closes for winter, opens again... you get the picture. If it's actually open when you're passing (and it's much more likely in the summer months) it's well worth a visit. For a quid you get a handful of big old pennies to spend on mechanical gypsy fortune tellers, What the Butler Saw machines and more besides. Sadly the kids can't play 'Win a Ciggie' any more but they will enjoy the early pinball-style games and watching the vicar being haunted in his graveyard. A perfect slice of old-school seaside charm.

THE VOLK'S RAILWAY

Easter until mid-autumn   *www.volkselectricrailway.co.uk*

The Volk's opened on August 4th 1883, making it the oldest electric railway in the world (you'll find it in *Guinness World Records*, sandwiched between the world's biggest pair of shoes and a photo of a man with four-metre long fingernails).

On its official opening day the railway's creator, Magnus Volk, invited a number of civic dignitaries for the first ride but, owing to their combined weight (civic dignitaries were notoriously portly in those days), they managed to break one of the planked pedestrian crossings that ran across the track. The train's first ever journey came to an undignified halt and the dignitaries were unloaded, to the jeers of a group of hostile cabbies, who believed it would take away their custom. They really needn't have worried.

The Sealife Centre

Marine Parade, opposite Brighton Pier
(01273) 604234
Mon-Fri 10am-5pm Sat-Sun 10am-6pm
Prices: it's complicated. Expect to pay £10-
£15 for an adult ticket.
www.visitsealife.com

When we think back to our very first review of the Sealife Centre in 1999 (*"a couple of kippers and a dead dog floating in the shark tank"*) it's hard to believe how much this place has been transformed. Once a shabby and embarrassing tourist attraction, the Sealife Centre is now nothing short of sensational. And while its prices are not for the faint-hearted (take the whole family and you'll be eating gravel for the week), whether you're entertaining the kids or looking for somewhere unusual for a blind date, you will not be disappointed. Housed inside a cavernous Victorian building, the Sealife Centre is packed with a whole range of European sea life in huge tanks, and offers feeding opportunities, glimpses "inside the lab" where stuff is nurtured and grown, and a Jules Verne Nautilus room where you can look down on the sharks and Lulu (the marine turtle, not the pint-sized Scottish singer).

And, of course, the payoff at the end is the underwater tunnels where you get to see them all swimming overhead. *"Look it's waving,"* said nephew Alex on our last visit, as a stingray flapped by.

But that's only just the beginning of your adventures – other sections include Sea Serpents and Amazonia, a cross between a hall of mirrors, the Eden Project and a dimly-lit tropical fish shop. If you've got very young kids, be warned, they *might* find this genuinely scary in a hiding-behind-the-settee-while-*Dr Who*-is-on kind of way. They are also prone to walk into the mirrors – which is entertaining to watch, provided it's not your own kids.
Top tip: book online for cheaper tickets.

Fishing Museum

201 Kings Road Arches (01273) 723064
9am-6pm Admission free
brightonfishingmuseum.org.uk

Worth a visit if you're wandering between the piers. There's a beautiful old fishing boat in the centre of the exhibition, plenty of ephemera, old photos and memorabilia from Regency days. They even do Punch and Judy shows during the summer holidays.

ARTY FARTY

The Phoenix Gallery
10-14 Waterloo Place (01273) 603700
Wed-Sun 11am-5pm
Admission free
phoenixarts.org

Over the past thirty years the Phoenix Gallery has transformed from a squat to a thriving art gallery with exhibitions changing on a regular basis. They also organise a wide range of workshops, ranging from tapestry and ceramics to Super-8 moviemaking, and run open days where you can have a nose round the artists' studios.

Fabrica
40 Duke Street (01273) 778646
Opening times vary
Closed Dec-April (it's too cold!)
Admission free
fabrica.org.uk

This converted church is a gallery space for installations and contemporary art, and is an essential drop-in spot when visiting the Lanes in summer. They do four main shows a year, offering the public a chance to see new commissioned works from artists who over the years have done everything from growing a wildflower meadow to hanging a rainbow of shirts.

The Artists' Quarter
Kings Road Arches

Down on the seafront between the two piers and below the kissing sculpture, this small stretch of the beach has been home for twenty years now to a collection of local artists whose colourful workshops and galleries are permanently on display to the public. Originally owned by fishermen, these little rooms would once have been used for descaling fish (to be sold where the carousel now stands), which accounts for the occasional odd whiff. Open all year round, even in the most improbable gales, this is London gallery quality at half the price, with work ranging from cards and paintings to exotic furniture and puppets.

Artists' open Houses

Brighton (and Hove) has probably more artists per square metre than anywhere else in the known universe. Every May and December you can go and nose around their houses and gardens when they hold free weekend mini-exhibitions, known collectively as the Artists' Open Houses. Hundreds of houses, artists and craftspeople are involved. Most houses are grouped geographically into Trails, which originally had their own brochures. They are now all gathered together into one handy brochure, with maps. As well as the visual arts (paintings, drawings, prints and sculpture) you'll also find ceramics, furniture, jewellery, stained glass, clothing, cards and more on sale direct from the artist or designer at cheaper-than-gallery prices.

The oldest Trail is Fiveways, named after the road junction, which started in 1982 when Ned Hoskins (109 Stanford Avenue) opened his house to the public during the Brighton Festival. This Trail also has the distinction of its own pub, the Open House, on Springfield Road. Over the railway tracks, south of London Road station, is Beyond the Level, founded in 1996. Trails further afield include Rottingdean, Prestonville, Hove, Portslade and Shoreham, while in the middle of the city are Central Brighton Artists, The Hartington Trail, Hanover Art Trail, and Seven Dials Artists.

One outstanding feature of the Open Houses is the cake. Many houses offer home-made refreshments of a high standard, often in their gardens. Best house for cake is Kate Osborne's house at 32 Stanford Avenue, part of Fiveways, and the best place for Open House virgins (but no cake) is The Dragonfly House, 48 Ditchling Rise (Beyond the Level). The houses do change from year to year, so check the brochure or www.aoh.org.uk before setting out.

Make sure you add your address to their guest books when you visit: that way you'll be invited to next year's private view and be given lots of wine. Or try your chances on the Friday night before the first weekend on May.

Alan (Fred) Pipes

Introducing the first (legal) distillery in the city of Brighton...

GIN
DISTILLED-BESIDE-THE-SEASIDE®

Brighton is the Pavilion, the Pier and the Duke of York's. It's the Prince Regent, Laurence Olivier and Max Miller. It's Phoebe Hessel, Mrs Fitzherbert and Martha Gunn. It's Brighton & Hove (actually), Mods & Rockers and the Seagulls. It's the Veteran Car Run, the London to Brighton and Brighton Races. It's the Downs, the sea and Brighton Rock. It's Pride, naughty weekends, illicit pleasures and now...it's Brighton Gin

www.brightongin.com

Twitter: @BrightonGin - Instagram: @distilled_beside_the_seaside - Facebook: BrightonGin

The spotter's guide to

In 2000 the Brighton and Hove Bus Company had the idea of daubing the names of more than 50 famous people with local connections on their buses, giving celebrity spotting in this town a whole new twist.

No longer are you obliged to spend two hours in the rain outside the Brighton Centre just to catch a glimpse of Bono's knobbly knees. All you need now is a pencil, a copy of this guide and a rudimentary knowledge of public transport. Just five minutes on Western Road and you could see Norman Cook, Winston Churchill or even Leo Sayer streak by and nearly knock you over.

We've only included our favourite fifteen here, but serious spotters can find the rest listed at *www.buses.co.uk*.

When you've spotted all fifteen tear out this page, send it to us with all the boxes neatly filled in, and the first five we receive will each win a special Cheeky cagoule and a year's subscription to *Guardian Soulmates*.

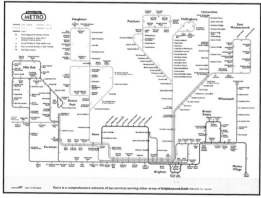

The territory of the Brighton & Hove bus

Brighton & Hove buses

- *Phil Starr* (Bus number 439) – younger brother of Ringo and the original drummer in the Beatles
- *Lord Olivier* (817) – grumpy kipper-obsessed luvvie
- *Jimmy Edwards* (648) – dead comedian with a moustache big enough to hide loaves of bread in
- *Wendy Richard* (450) – perpetually fascinated by Mrs Slocombe's pussy
- *Adam Faith* (649) – hiccuppy singer responsible for discovering Leo Sayer (down the back of his sofa)
- *Sir Winston Churchill* (550) – The Greatest Briton Ever (as voted by the great British public) whose policies included "experimenting with chemical weapons on Arabs" and "the sterilisation of the feeble-minded"
- *Eric Gill* (663) – Ditchling-based artist who kindly provided the typeface for this book
- *Derek Jameson* (478) – inventor of the famous whisky
- *Rudyard Kipling* (935) – you've eaten the cakes, now read the book
- *Prince Regent* (402) – a swimming pool in town*
- *Charles Busby* (456) – small yellow man who spent much of his time hanging precariously from telegraph wires
- *John Nash* (433) – celebrated country-and-western singer, whose hit *A Cowboy from Whitehawk Buggered up my Patio* made him a superstar. We think.
- *Stanley Deason* (428) – one-time maverick mayor who, in the early 70s, elected Frank Zappa as the King of Hove
- *Sir Arthur Conan Doyle* (675) – gave 100p haircuts at 21B Baker Street
- *Charles Dickens* (551) – had a mate who knew someone in Brighton

The male and female of the species

AMAZING BUS FACTS

- Often seen gathering in flocks at Churchill Square or North St.

- Predators: trucks and taxis.

- Prey: Cyclists, dozy tourists and prams.

*not sure why this one is here.

ANIMAL MAGIC
& The Great Outdoors

BEASTS

Dolphin and seal spotting
seawatchfoundation.org.uk

There has been an increase in sightings of dolphins along the south coast, in particular bottlenose dolphins and harbour porpoises. To spot one is rare but the best time to see them is high tide between March and September. Between the two piers and around the Marina are your best viewing spots, and the Seawatch website is there to help with identification. The most celebrated dolphin ever seen in Brighton was dubbed Smurfy because of his unusual iridescent colouring (and large white floppy hat). If you do see one (a dolphin, not a Smurf) submit your sighting to the website above; they're tracking all dolphin, whale and seal activity along the British coast.

Rockpooling

Past the Marina on the Undercliff Walk to Rottingdean you'll find some good rockpools with edible spider and shore crabs, sea anemones and other saltwater goodies. If you're in the car, just follow the coastal road heading towards Eastbourne. From Brighton Pier it's ten minutes to cycle or 30 minutes to walk.

Llama trekking

Ashdown Forest Llama Park
Wych Cross, East Sussex
(01825) 712040
Prices start at £20 per llama
www.llamapark.co.uk

Every couple of years or so the llama farm seems to change location. Once it was on the Downs and now it's drifted all the way to Ashdown Forest, which means it shouldn't really merit inclusion in a book about Brighton but as we're suckers for something a bit out of the ordinary, we've decided to overlook the fact.

And for lovers of large hairy quadrupeds what better way to spend an afternoon than taking a stroll with one of these gentle creatures? Worth noting is that you can only *walk* with the llamas, not sit on them. And galloping around the woods on them naked is right out.

Shepherding

(01273) 292929
Lookerer courses run Aug-Oct
www.brighton-hove.gov.uk

If you've ever fancied standing around on the Downs with a piece of straw stuck between your teeth while tending your flock, Brighton Council now has its own sheep and welcomes volunteer shepherds (known as 'lookerers'). It's free and you can apply by phoning the number above or checking out the council website. If selected you'll be sent on a one-day training course at Stanmer Park to learn about sheep ailments, legal aspects of grazing, and how to ward off randy Welshmen.

Once qualified you'll be required to give up one hour a week to keep a check on your flock, though the temptation to stand around all day in a smock shouting "get orf my land" at ramblers and paragliders will, we're sure, be overwhelming.

The Spider-Cat

Halfway up a wall
Tue-Sat 11am-11.30am
Admission free
www.thespidercatis.com

Scaling the wall on the corner of a building on the Old Steine, close to the entrance of Pool Valley, there's a small black cat that's been there almost forever. Rumour has it that it's a witch who had a heart attack midway through her animal transmogrification process and became as the stone she clung to. Local wiccans frequently gather here in homage, though as it's very close to a bus stop they may simply be off on a trip to the country to gather enchanted moss or something.

BIRDS

The starlings
Between the piers, one hour before sunset

Only the most hard-boiled individual could fail to be moved by this spectacular display of nature at its most mysterious. Brighton's long-established murmurations of starlings now seem most focussed on the Palace Pier instead of the derelict West Pier, a result of their predilection for candy floss. Every autumn and winter evening at dusk more than 50,000 of these beautiful shining creatures congregate in an amorphous swooping mass. It is truly astonishing. And nobody really knows why they do it. Dedicated watchers swear that at the winter solstice the birds briefly take the form of Phil Collins in the twilit heavens and tweet out a wobbly rendition of *Sussudio*, but this is of course nonsense. It's clearly *In The Air Tonight*.

RSPB
(01273) 775333

Apart from the gulls, pigeons, starlings and occasional curio in local parks, you'll have to get out of Brighton to enjoy some really good twitching but there's plenty on offer in surrounding areas. You'll find purple sandpipers at the Marina, a whole host of rarities regularly blown in at Beachy Head, and an RSPB reserve forty minutes away in Pulborough. And if watching aggressive herring gulls who steal chips and rip bins apart is your hobby, you've come to the right town.

WHERE TO TAKE A GOOD STROLL

Recommended reading

There is a remarkably useful and entertaining little book, written by some astoundingly good-looking people, that provides a range of guided walks both in Brighton and out in the surrounding rural and semi-rural environs, each walk having a specific and sometimes slightly silly theme. By striking coincidence it has a similar name to the book you are reading now, being titled *Cheeky Walks in Brighton and Sussex,* available in good bookshops or from *cheekyguides.com*, apparently. But if you're too mean-spirited to shell out for that and don't mind that our kids will be eating limpet gruel again for tea, here are a few more economical ideas below.

The Marina Breakwater

Down near the marina is a breakwater that extends for about a quarter of a mile out to sea. Go when the sea's a bit rough and it can be a delightfully hairy experience. It'll take you about twenty minutes to walk there from Brighton/ Palace Pier, and ideally you should try and time it for sunset. Then you could stick around in the marina for a drink (bad idea) or walk back into town and flop around at the Basketmakers pub (good idea).

The Undercliff Walk to Rottingdean

From Brighton Pier head to the Marina, find the undercliff path behind Asda, keep going and you'll reach Rottingdean in about an hour. Most of the path from the Marina onwards has been carved out of the imposing chalky cliffs which, together with the magnificent views of the sea, make this walk fairly spectacular. And it's good by bike too as it's completely flat. As you approach Rottingdean you'll start to chance upon rockpools and little coves where people go winkle picking and crab fishing.

Rottingdean is, in contrast to Brighton, one of those classic seaside villages with old-fashioned shops and boutiques. One particular shop, The Cabin (sadly long gone), is said to have been the inspiration behind the Local Shop in *The League of Gentlemen*. Years ago someone emailed to tell us:

"I went in to buy a copy of The Guardian *and the woman said defensively,* 'Oh no. We only stock local papers in here…'"

Once you've had a good nose around the village you'll need to head back to Brighton, though if you can't face doing the walk again buses do run regularly back to town.

This really is one of the best and most accessible local walks, whatever the season. In summer there's a café halfway (the coffee is instant but the cakes are nice), while in winter you may have your head blown off but if you wrap up warm you can treat yourself to a mulled wine in the White Horse which overlooks the sea.

Glynde to Lewes

Take the train to Glynde and follow the stunning but straightforward walk back over Mount Caburn to Lewes. You can't go wrong (there's nowhere else to walk), you won't see a soul, the scenery is spectacular and when you drop down the hill into Lewes, you are only a short walk from the Gardeners Arms for a cheeky pint and a pickled egg.

The Indian Chattri on the Downs

High up on a hill overlooking Brighton is one the town's most curious memorials, built to commemorate the thousands of Indians who died in Brighton during the First World War. They were brought here because the Royal Pavilion was at that time used as a hospital for the wounded – on the grounds that the soldiers would feel more at home there. Despite these rather misplaced good intentions, the wounded were more than a little bemused at having been stationed in what looked like an oriental brothel and, of course, bringing Sikhs and Hindus from every caste together under one roof meant the atmosphere was not always convivial.

The Chattri memorial was built on the site of the ghat (funeral pyre) for 53 of those soldiers and opened in 1921, and an annual visit is still made by the High Commissioner for India.

Take the A23 out of Brighton, follow the A273 to Hassocks and go through Pyecombe. Take a right down Mill Lane and follow until you reach the windmill carpark.

From the carpark go past the Old Barn Farm and golf course, and keep following the path until you reach a signpost. Go through the gate, keep the large clump of trees on your right and follow the South Downs Way. It's probably best to take an OS map as these directions come from some illegible notes we scribbled years ago and it's easy to miss the Chattri, hidden by trees until the last minute. The reference is TQ304111.

There are also maps available from Brighton tourist information centres.

OPEN-AIR POOLS

Saltdean Lido

Saltdean Park Road, Saltdean
Opening times uncertain at present,
summer weekends most likely
www.saltdeanlido.co.uk

It is a miracle that this original open-air art deco swimming pool (one of only three in the entire country) still survives. Completely restored in 1998, it was again neglected and then rescued from redevelopment in 2012, and is now run by a community-interest company who are trying to get it back on its feet. Only a fifteen-minute drive from Brighton, this is the place to don your best knee-length striped woollen bathing costume and parade around with a Martini in hand.

Pells Pool at Lewes

Brook Street, Lewes (01273) 472334
Open every day May to September
Adults £4 kids £2
pellspool.org.uk

This little-known open-air swimming pool in Lewes lays claim to being the oldest freshwater public pool in the country. There's plenty of space for sunbathing on the grass on warm days (and why would you go any other time?) and the pool itself is large enough to get some decent lengths in before undoing all that good work with a bacon sarnie and white chocolate Magnum.

GAME

28

29 You sing 'Do you really want to hurt me?' in front of some mono-browed slapheads at the karaoke bar and get beaten up

30 finish

21

20

19 You fall into a deep slumber on the world's dullest ghost train

16

17

18

9 You jump off the pier and drown

8

7

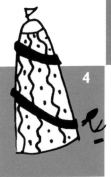

4

5

6 The arcade swallows your kids for two hours allowing you to slope off for a crafty pint

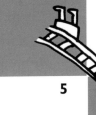

The Sea

Despite the fact that Brighton receives millions of visitors every year, you'd be surprised how few take the plunge and venture – beyond the occasional paddle – into the sea. Is it too cold, is it fear of sharks, jellyfish, toilet paper, or are you all just a big bunch of jessies? In an effort to encourage a few more of you out of the pubs and into the Blue, this chapter gives the facts about seawater quality and explores a few ways to go messing about in the water.

WHERE TO SWIM

Brighton Beach

A lot of people are sniffy about swimming in the sea in Brighton, but floating on your back in the water, gently bobbing around while the sun turns your skin the texture of a Chesterfield still rates as one of our favourite Brighton experiences. And while on the hottest days of the year the beach can be packed to the hilt with holidaymakers and half the town skiving off work, you'll still have most of the sea to yourself.

MCS*: Recommended

Hove Beach

A lot quieter than Brighton and fringed by lawns, benches, grand Regency seafront buildings and charming multi-coloured £500,000 beach huts to have a good old nose into as you stroll casually past in your Speedos.

MCS: Recommended

*Marine Conservation Society water quality rating

Portslade/Southwick Beach

On the other side of Hove Lagoon with a romantic backdrop of industrial buildings and a gas-fired power station is this unofficial naturist beach. Unlike the official nudist beach in Brighton you are actually allowed to keep your clothes on though like Brighton nudist beach you still might spot the odd gentleman in a state of 'excitement'.
MCS: Recommended

Shoreham Beach

Seven miles west and just beyond Shoreham harbour you'll find a remarkably clean and peaceful beach with real sand! And if you get a bit peckish, there's sea kale growing near the high-tide line.
MCS: Not tested

Saltdean

Go a couple of miles east of the Marina for this low key and family friendly stretch of sand and shingle. Fresh sand was brought in to "recharge" the beach in the 90s so there is now a rather large hole in the ground next to the donkey rides at Skegness,
MCS: Recommended

Brighton Watersports

185 Kings Road Arches (01273) 323160
All year round (for retail) 10am until
"whenever"
£10 per person per hour for kayak rental
www.thebrightonwatersports.co.uk

Found under the promenade
between the two piers, these fellows
hire out single and tandem kayaks
and stand-up paddleboards. They also
hire wetsuits, have changing rooms
and showers, and sell beachwear and
wakeboarding gear. Kayaking round
the piers on a warm summer's day,
watching the cormorants nesting at
the back of the West Pier and seeing
Brighton from the sea has got to be
one of the best tenners you'll ever
spend. Highly recommended.

Lagoon Watersports

Western end of Hove promenade
(01273) 424842
Late spring to autumn
www.lagoon.co.uk

Windsurfing, sailing, yachting and
powerboating start at £69 for a two-
hour lesson with an instructor. Their
latest activity, stand-up paddleboarding,
is proving to be quite a hit too.

Yellowave Beachsports

299 Madeira Drive (opp. the Concorde 2)
(01273) 672222
www.yellowave.co.uk

A rare chance to get sand between
your toes at these twin beach
volleyball courts which have been a
fantastic addition to Brighton seafront.
There's a very welcoming vibe down
here; if you've never played before
you can get lessons, join a beginners
group and hang out afterwards with a
beer at the café.

Brighton Swimming Club

www.brightonsc.co.uk

Based at Arch 250E near
Brighton Pier, this is the England's
longest-established swimming
club, formed in 1860 and
still going strong. Many of its
hardcore club members meet
every morning at 7.30 for a dip
before work. Only if the sea
"looks suicidal" will they give it a
miss. New members are always
welcome but are required to
wear a coloured rubber cap
when going in, which might make
you feel like a right charlie but is
for your own safety.

Those members who brave
the sea when it's below 40° –
something that only happens
occasionally – can pride
themselves on being issued with
a club certificate. The late club
member Jim Wild, who made it
to the ripe old age of 92, used to
recall the time the temperature
of the sea dropped to below 30°
and he returned to the club with
icicles hanging from his nipples!
Annual traditions include a big
game of water polo down at the
Marina, a chilly annual Christmas
dip and a Boxing Day race.

SURFING

*By shaggy Hawaiian-shirt-wearing blond
Marcus O'Dair*

Let's face it, Brighton is no surfer's
paradise; the waves are infrequent,
small and messy, the sea can be dirty
and the temperatures would send
an Inuit running for extra thermal
undies. As the title of a film about the
Brighton surf scene noted, it's
Not California.

But Brighton surfers, many of
whom have surfed all over the world,
are passionate about the local breaks.
Yes, the waves are usually small, but
they're good enough for several
competition-winning Brighton surfers
who are out there every chance they
get. Yes, it's cold, but people surf in the
Outer Hebrides, in Sweden, even in
Alaska (the boundary between surfing
and masochism being decidedly
blurred).

The main spots

The two main local breaks are the
Hot Pipes and the Marina. The Hot
Pipes, near Shoreham Power Station,
has a friendly atmosphere and, for
once in Brighton, easy parking. This
fairly gentle beachbreak is a good
spot for beginners.

The Marina, on the other hand,
is ridden mainly by shortboarders.
It's a fairly fast wave breaking over
a shallow chalk-and-flint reef, and
suitable for more experienced surfers
only. It used to have a reputation as
a fairly heavy locals' spot and it's still
a good idea to show a bit of respect
for the regulars.

Other spots include the West Pier
(especially on a groundswell), the
Wedge (primarily a bodyboarding
break) and Shoreham Harbour.
Outside Brighton, check out
Littlehampton and Eastbourne and,
farther afield, East and West Wittering
and Camber Sands.

Shopping

Brighton can be a shopaholic's paradise, particularly for lovers of antiques, fashion, jewellery, music, kitsch, glamourwear, retro clothing and bird whistles. And with more than 400 independent shops in the centre alone, the town boasts more unique boutiques per square mile than anywhere else in the UK. The most colourful areas with the best shops are definitely North Laine, Kemptown and the Old Lanes. For the less adventurous, Western Road and the Churchill Square shopping centre have everything that you'd expect to find in a high street (including crowds, concrete and speeding bus drivers).

North Laine is terrific, not only for its wide selection of 60s/70s clothes and record shops but also for odditiess like Vegetarian Shoes and Pussy. Get into the swing of North Laine and you'll find yourself going home with a woolly mammoth ivory nose-stud, a mod suit and a pair of thigh-high boots. And you only popped out for a loaf of bread.

Kemptown has an eclectic mix of emporia including flea markets, antique shops, gay clothing stores, poodle parlours and over a hundred outlets stocking butt-plugs and lube. The Lanes, while a lot less flamboyant than North Laine, are good for jewellery (particularly if trying to track down your great aunt's stolen necklace), cafés and new clothes shops. Think of it this way: if North Laine was Bjork the Old Lanes would be Elaine Page (with Kemptown as Shirley Bassey).

And finally, before you rush off with your credit cards, don't get up too early! Shops here can open notoriously late (especially in North Laine) and not always at the same time every morning. So, do yourself a favour, have a night on the tiles and get up at the same time as nearly everyone else here – around 10am.

The Punker Bunker

Below Immediate Clothing, Sydney Street
Mon-Sun 11am-6pm

Run by Just One Life promoter Buz, this tiny basement shop caters for anyone with a passion for ska, 2 Tone, metal, rock and underground punk rock. Hanging on to those old punk rock ethics, Buz is an eager promoter of live, noisy music in Brighton, and sells all his CDs for a tenner or less. He used to play certain records to discourage the nu-metal kids from visiting his shop, and is glad that the fad is now over. You can also buy tickets for all punk-related gigs down here, buy yourself a badge that says Fuck Off, find adverts for local bands and learn all about the scene from Buz. Long may he reign.

Monkey Music Emporium

43 Baker Street
Mon-Sat 10am-6pm

Just off London Road, this place is worth the trek from the town centre. Though specialising in Krautrock, owner Mark stocks a wide range of records, mostly rock and jazz and mostly vinyl, and you'll go bananas (sorry) for their prices with singles at 50p, £1 for classical records, and most others starting at £3. The walls are covered in rarities and mint-condition originals, going for anything from £50 to £250 for an original Help! LP. Mark also stocks a range of used amps and turntables for those whose parents have already thrown theirs away.

The Record Album
8 Terminus Road (01273) 323853
Mon-Sat 11am-4.30pm
www.therecordalbum.com

Up the hill just round the corner from Brighton Station lies The Record Album: the oldest record shop in the country and a must for collectors of rare vinyl.

The shop specialises in all types of deleted recordings and one-offs, especially soundtrack albums. Most stock is new or in mint condition, and the records that owner George sticks up in his shop window invariably reflect whatever movies are being shown on terrestrial TV that week. Don't expect to find a bargain: prices start around £10 and go up to £75 or more for that ultra-rare electronic 50s sci-fi B movie soundtrack. George also supplies records to the BBC, theatre and radio and has a mail-order service. It is easy to spend a couple of hours here, simply for the company of its owner – George is impeccably polite and happy to share

his passion for music with you. Though ask him why he doesn't stock CDs and George will shudder and say, *"uh, those ghastly little frisbees."*

One Stop Records
30 Sydney Street
(above Wolf & Gypsy Vintage)

An absolutely minuscule shop, selling both new and used dance, house, disco, jazz, soul and reggae. Given such a small space, owner Chris is *"very choosy"* with his stock. As a member of the neo-disco band Soft Rocks, Chris obviously knows his stuff, and the result is a fresh and interesting selection.

The Wax Factor
24 Trafalgar Street (01273) 673744
Mon-Fri 10.15am-5.30pm, Sat 9.45am-5.30pm
www.thewaxfactor.com

There is an unwritten law in Brighton that all good record shops are run by blokes called Alan. The good news is The Wax Factor is not only run by Alan Senior, who has been in the business 30 years and is a mine of information on everything you ever wanted (or didn't want) to know about rare vinyl, but his son Alan Junior trades here too. Alantastic!

CDs are on sale but it is the vast stock of (mainly) 50s to 70s vinyl that is so impressive: the walls are adorned with extremely rare and very tempting records from bygone days, many of which could cost you a kidney or two.

Sure, they know the value of what they've got but there are bargains to be had and they frequently clear out stock for a quid upwards. The two Als will also keep you abreast of new stock if they know your tastes, no matter how rare or bizarre, though they draw the line at animal porn and Sting records.

City Books

23 Western Road (01273) 725306
Mon-Sat 9.30am-6pm, Sun 11am-4.30pm
www.city-books.co.uk

Brighton's biggest independent bookshop and the kind of place you wander into to buy the latest McEwan, end up having a natter with owners Paul or Inge and find half the day has gone. City Books cares about its customers and makes an extra-special effort in properly representing Brighton through its choice of stock and window displays. They're also responsible for putting on many of the city's most interesting literary events, whether it's David Sedaris telling stories in the Pavilion or Will Self reading from his latest book *My Obstreperous and Guignol Coruscation.*

City Books have been twice shortlisted for the Independent Bookshop of the Year award and rightly so. In an age where Amazon dominates the book world, places like City Books deserve our undying love and support.

Colin Page

36 Duke Street (01273) 325954
Mon-Sat 9am-5.30pm

This former 19th century baker's is officially Brighton's oldest bookshop and comes complete with all the trappings of the dusty, antiquated variety once frequented by JR Hartley, including a marvellous old spiral staircase at the back. Set up in 1975 by John Loska and his twin brother Stephen, the shop specialises in antiquated and rare books but, for the general buyer, always has a box of interesting paperbacks outside and

SHOPPING

Inge and Paul of City Books celebrate 30 glorious years of paper cuts and inky fingers

a basement of hardback fiction and factual books ranging from history to the occult. It's also a popular haunt when the luvvies are in town. The likes of Stephen Fry and Simon Callow are regulars, as are old-school politicians ("the ones who still read," quipped Stephen). A treat for the serious book collector.

Dave's Comics

5 Sydney Street (01273) 691012
Mon-Fri 10am-6pm, Wed 11am-7pm,
Sat 9:30am-6pm, Sun 11am-5pm
www.davescomics.co.uk

As well as being comic nerd heaven on earth, Dave's breaks a 21st century rule by often offering cheaper prices than the Internet. They sell the latest comic book releases upstairs, while the ground floor is dedicated to a staggering range of graphic novels and art books. Knowledgeable staff can guide you in your selection or order

obscurities, whether your interest lies in local indie publications (including Brighton: The Graphic Novel), European comics, manga, gift books, memorabilia or posters. There's also a smaller shop two doors down, just called Dave's, with an extensive selection of back issues, as well as collectible figurines and action figures, and a massive range of board games. The atmosphere in both shops is studious and lending library silent, which may be because Brighton's impecunious comic fans often come here to read the stuff they can't afford to buy.

Magazine Brighton

22 Trafalgar Street (01273) 687968
Tues-Fri 11am-5pm, Sat 10am-6pm,
Sun 12noon-4pm
magazinebrighton.com

At Cheeky Towers we are acutely aware that the days of making actual profit from printed books are long gone. As such, we're now forced to live in the utility cupboard at a friend's mum's just to keep producing the books our tens of readers know and love. Despite the (very real) crisis in publishing, there has of late been a surprising resurgence of beautifully-made independent magazines across the west, with a particular focus on travel, craft and hobbies, and favouring names like Flow, Toast, Drift, Monocle, Cuticle, Victory, Cornflake and Blancmange.

Magazine Brighton stock an ever-expanding selection of such titles (over 250 to date), carefully chosen by owner Martin and presented in a simple, elegant style that echoes the aesthetic of the magazines themselves. Our current favourite is Ernest, packed with history, travelogues, etymology and features that range from the story of denim to ghost villages.

Kemptown Bookshop

91 St George's Road (01273) 682110
Mon-Sat 9am-5.30pm
www.kemptownbookshop.co.uk
www.bookroomartpress.co.uk

One of only two remaining independent bookshops left in the city, Kemptown Bookshop has been here for more than 40 years, and run by the affable Darion Goodwin for the past twenty. Charming, personable and peaceful, this is the very antithesis of Black Books, you'll never find its owner drunkenly throwing books at customers or accidentally setting fire to himself. Instead, priding themselves on a fast-order service, Kemptown Bookshop guarantee next-day delivery for 90% of orders or a free pint and cheesy chips from the Barley Mow next door.

Also worth a note is the Bookroom Art Press, another of Darion's ventures, which offers a variety of beautiful limited-edition prints from such artists as John Nash, Eric Ravilious and Vanessa Bell, which can be seen framed around the shop.

The Wax Factor

24 Trafalgar Street (01273) 673744
Mon-Fri 10.15am-5.30pm, Sat 9.45am-5.30pm
www.thewaxfactor.com

If second-hand books on the occult, drugs, philosophy, sci-fi, eastern mysticism and music are your bag then this is the place for you. The window display alone should be enough to pull you in as you drool over all the Crowley, Philip K Dick and Burroughs books. They have a pretty good selection of general fiction here too, which is just on your right as you enter. More importantly perhaps, they stock one of the best collections of second-hand CDs and vinyl in Brighton, with seven-inches and CD singles in the basement (See Record Shops).

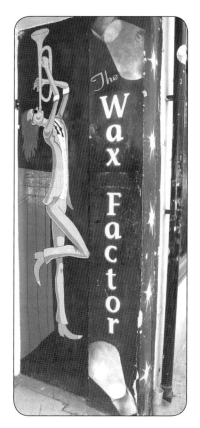

Waterstones

71-74 North Street (01273) 206017
Mon-Fri 9am-7pm, Sat 9am-6pm,
Sun 11am-5pm
www.waterstones.co.uk

The Brighton branch of Waterstones has always felt more like a friendly local bookstore than a chain. Much of its success is down to its lovely staff, who work hard to ensure that their stock, as far as possible, reflects the true spirit of the town. Many seem to have their finger on the pulse of what Brighton readers are looking for, demonstrating that with a little care and passion, a chainstore can still have a heart.

GROOVY GIFTS AND COOL THINGS FOR THE HOME

Blackout

53 Kensington Place
(01273) 671741
Mon-Sat 10am-6pm, Sun 11am-5pm
www.blackout-uk.com

Off the beaten track in North Laine, Blackout still gets long-term Brightonians stumbling through the doorway for the first time going *"ooh, are you new?"*, despite having been here for more than twenty years.

The shop's unique angle is kitsch-fashion-folk art and religious imagery and it has cornered the market in Tibetan baby carriers, fluorescent loo brushes, Virgin Mary ashtrays, plastic Hindu gods, recycled-tyre tables and tribal jewellery.

Their original policy, and namesake, of selling nothing black seems to have been dropped in recent years, as our casual enquiries were met with *"it's a long story…"*

Castor & Pollux

165 King's Road Arches, Lower Promenade (01273) 773776
Mon-Sun 10am-5pm
www.castorandpollux.co.uk

Named after the Roman gods of seafarers, C&P is an attractive beach-house boutique selling stylish books (*The Girl's Guide to Surfing* anyone?), furniture, art, flowers, pottery and (increasingly) beautiful prints from artists such as Quentin Blake and Rob Ryan.

Owner Mike clearly has a taste for quality; more places like this down on the seafront please!

In My Room

35 Gloucester Road (01273) 675506
Tues-Fri 9.30am-5.30pm, Sat 9am-6pm,
Sun 11am-4.30 pm
www.inmyroom.co.uk

No evil volcanic fortress would be complete without a 1960s G-Plan swivel armchair - as popularised by James Bond's nemesis, Blofeld. Thankfully In My Room stocks this essential (POA, white cat not included) alongside other high-end 20th century furniture, objects and art prints. The designs, from the likes of Eames, Merrow Associates, and Ercol, have a modern feel, and despite being fifty years old all the pieces have been lovingly restored. Owner Ollie also has a penchant for vintage Space Age design, including spherical Keracolor televisions, lipstick mirrors and flip clocks, and makes sure to stock "fun things" like resin dinosaurs and wooden toy trucks.

McCready Bags

47 Upper North Street 07971 176554
Mon-Fri 11am-6pm, Sat 11am-4pm

Alistair started making his own bags after purchasing one made of old curtains from an Oxfam in Cologne and thinking, "I could do that." Thirty years later he now has hundreds of unique bags made on the sewing machine in his shop. From small purses for £6 to larger handbags (£30-£40), all are lovingly handmade with beautiful (and vibrantly patterned) fabric sourced from his native Liverpool and French markets. It's the details which really make these bags special, from the linings to printed "with love from Brighton" labels. Worth a visit just to chat about Brighton, bags and life. Alistair hopes to start a website and one of those *"blobs"* everyone's on about, if he could only get the computer working.

Painting Pottery Café

31 North Road (01273) 628952
Tues-Sat 10.30am-6.30pm, Sun 11am-6pm,
Weds late-night session, booking required
www.paintingpotterycafe.co.uk

As well as holding workshops where children and adults can learn to throw pots and make clay sculptures, you can try your hand here at decorating plates, mugs, eggcups and tiles. They will ply you with coffee, hot chocolate and teas and will even glaze and fire your finished masterpieces. The late-night Wednesday sessions are especially worth attending, as you can bring your own booze. So, men, don't be surprised if after fourteen cans of Special Brew you wake to find eight new eggcups sitting on your kitchen table, each crudely adorned with pictures of your own genitalia.

Pardon My French

15 St George's Road (01273) 694479
Mon-Sat 10am-5pm
www.pardonmyfrench.co.uk

A cornucopia of luxurious boudoiresque items created by our garlic-loving friends over the seas and specially selected by owners Stephanie and Sandra. The whole shop is jam-packed with objets from French nightwear and Provençal plates to old enamel signs with such messages as "Chat Gentil", "Lapin Lunatique" or (our favourite) "Attention! Chien Bizarre".

Top tip: if you visit the shop wearing a beret and carrying a string of onions they give you a special discount. If that's all you're wearing however, you might get arrested.

Cuddly unthreatening Hattifatteners

Pussy

3a Kensington Gardens (01273) 604861
Mon-Sat 10am-6pm, Sun 11am-4pm
www.pussyhomeboutique.co.uk

Previous editions of this book expressed concern over owner Nicky's increasing obsession with all things Moomin. We can now report that her fanaticism has only risen, with Moomin-themed items now taking up a good three quarters of the shop space. Books, crockery, cutlery, towels, cushions, toys, clothing, cake tins, and cards- if you can put a Moomin on it, Nicky will stock it. While the range of erotic books and offensive greeting cards have been reduced as a result, there's still a good range of curious for the home including baby bunny lamps and teapots with eyes, and Tatty Devine jewellery.

Scandecor

20 Castle Street (01273) 820208
Mon-Sat 10am-5.30pm
www.artdeco-sofas.com

As the eagle-eyed reader may have spotted, this guide tends not to bother mentioning soft furnishings, those things that you spend half your life lolling about on. Step in here sir, I'm sorry, madam, and allow me to show you our range of Art Deco repro soft furniture, made to order in Brighton to designs created by buying originals and pulling them apart to see exactly how it was done. Been at it for over 40 years we have. Yes, they are utterly gorgeous aren't they? No, they don't cost any more than a bog-standard mass-produced one from a soulless industrial estate warehouse. We had that Martin Kemp in here the other day you know. Said he's never sat on a DFS sofa in his life...

Timeslip

90 Trafalgar Street
(01273) 609006
Open "eight days a week" 10am-6pm

Steering away from mainstream, big budget and blockbusters, friendly owner Mick has instead an excellent range of old classics (Hitchcock, Powell & Pressburger etc), cult movies and modern world cinema on DVD and video. And with prices ranging around the £3.50-£12 mark, anyone with good taste in films is going to find something here to take home and cherish.

Stretching their remit somewhat, Timeslip now also sells designer clothing, from Our Legacy, Albam and Comme des Garçons (£50-£200).

Velo Vitality

44 Trafalgar Street
(01273) 699184
Mon-Sat 10am-6pm
www.velovitality.co.uk

Selling a range of urban and classic bicycles, Velo Vitality caters for our active cycling scene with distinctively Brighton style. Tour de France hopefuls steer clear: husband and wife John and Jenny take a much more relaxed attitude to cycling. With a focus on comfort and leisure, their pastel vintage-style bikes will not only complement your new floral dress, but get you up even the steepest of Brighton hills.

With brands like Bobbin, Reid and Tokyobike for reasonable prices (£250-£550), Velo Vitality is great for beginners. They also stock a range of accessories (wicker baskets abound!) and provide a reliable repair service.

BOOZE, FAGS, SWEETS & FIREARMS

Bison Beer

7 East Street (01273) 809027
Mon-Sat 10am-7pm, Sun 11am-5pm
www.bisonbeer.co.uk

It's safe to say that the craft beer craze has a firm hold over Brighton, with specialist pubs popping up around every corner. However, few take it more seriously than best mates Jack and Nick, who have opened the city's first and only shop dedicated entirely to craft porters and ales. They stock an impressive 365+ varieties from local micro-breweries and around the world. For those who fancy joining these ranks, Bison also sell home brewing kits and run a brewing school at the Fishbowl pub opposite. Their most iconic products are the so-called 'Growlers'- 1.9L amber glass bottles which can be purchased for £10 and filled from one of four taps in-store. Thanks to a clever counter-pressure filling system, these vessels keep your beer fresh for up to six weeks. However, the best growler in the shop is the small dachshund, Henry, who lives under a bench and ensures that customers behave themselves.

Choccywoccydoodah

3 Meeting House Lane (01273) 329462
Mon-Sat 10am-6pm, Sun 11am-5pm
www.choccywoccydoodah.com

You'll forgive the ludicrous name the second you enter, take in that sweet smell of Belgian chocolate and marvel at the most outrageous, over-the-top chocolate cakes you've ever seen. They've got spiky fetish cakes, ones covered in realistic vegetables, ones with willies, roses, mermaids and more besides. If you can't afford a cake (their wedding cakes can cost £500 or more for a bespoke design) they do gold coins for under a fiver, with other economical choices including baby birds, moustaches, marshmallow lollies and solid chocolate dogs like Fifi the French bulldog. Head of Creativity here is the infamous Mr Dave Pop, also renowned for his kitsch songs and live appearances at various Brighton venues over the years. For the last few years Choccywoccy have even had their own reality TV show on the Good Food channel of which Dave, unsurprisingly, was the star attraction.

Cybercandy

15 Gardner Street 0845 838 0958
Mon-Fri 11am-6pm, Sat 10.30am-6.30pm,
Sun 11am-5pm
www.cybercandy.co.uk

This must surely be the only shop to have seven-year-old kids and 40 year

olds standing side by side, drooling over the items on display. Sweetie lovers, you'll think you've died and gone to heaven when you come here. With everything from retro classics Pez to special imports like almond M&Ms, banana Kit-Kats and peanut butter Twix, you'll be dreaming up a new spin on a classic bar before you even get to the till. Check out the far wall, where they've got more than 50 types of jelly bean, including Bertie Bott's vomit flavour.

If esoteric sweets are more your bag, you won't be disappointed with their Swedish Plopp bar or Danish Spunk gums, while lovers of the downright bizarre can tuck into scorpion lollies and chocolate-covered ants. And to think we spent our childhoods chewing on Fruit Salads and Blackjacks.

C&H Weston Ltd

12 East Street
(01273) 326338
Mon-Sat 9am-5.30pm,
Sun 10.30am-4.30pm
www.chweston.co.uk

Among the sea of over-priced clothes boutiques and jewellery shops in the Lanes these guys remain a curious anomaly. One of the oldest shops in Brighton, C&H Weston started out as a gunmaker's back in 1819 and while they no longer knock up firearms in the back room, they do stock a huge range of air rifles and pistols, as well as Barbour jackets and the like. While air guns start at £30 and go up to as much as £10,000, you can bag a plastic crow and magpie for a fiver or a giant-sized plastic owl for scaring away seagulls and mad aunties for £20.

NB: to buy an air rifle you need ID that proves you are over eighteen. To buy a Barbour jacket you will need to complete the Daily Telegraph crossword in less than ten minutes in front of the staff and have a braying laugh.

The Lanes Armoury
26 Meeting House Lane
(01273) 321357
Mon-Sat 11am-5pm
www.thelanesarmoury.co.uk

Souvenir firearms and armour from all periods of history. Get your granny that old Vickers submachine gun she always wanted or maybe a Luger for young cousin Donald. They also have Kentucky rifles, Zulu war shields, Napoleonic swords and even a helmet from the Iraq war. A Tudor suit of armour would set you back around £20,000, though the less affluent can buy a cap badge for only £3.

If the Ronnie Reagan picture isn't visible then nag them to get it back on display as there's a good story behind it.

Taylors Tobacconist
19 Bond Street (01273) 606110
Mon-Fri 10am-5.30pm, Sat 10am-6pm,
Sun 11am-6pm
taylors-tobacconist.co.uk

A THANK YOU FOR SMOKING sign welcomes you as you enter and the wide range of flavoured hand-rolling tobaccos (including chocolate), lighters and Cuban cigars reminds us why it took so long to kick such a pleasurable habit. Go on, have a fag.

"Point that thing at me and I'll be straight on the blower to the RSPB."

and has a huge cupboard of it for you to peruse, from cute twee and cartoon prints to luscious florals. Dig for Victory also create unique wedding and bridesmaid's dresses, for £250-£300, and have recently started making coats too.

Get Cutie

33 Kensington Gardens (01273) 687768
Mon-Fri 10.30am-5.30pm, Sat 10am-6pm,
Sun 11am-5pm
www.getcutie.co.uk

Celebrated for their beautiful prints depicting anything from cowgirls to gothic bats, Get Cutie specialises in handmade 50s-style creations: dresses, skirts and shirts that may be an occasional treat for those on student wages but won't break the bank for the tens of people on decent wages in Brighton.

And if you need a pair of knickers with pictures of the Eiffel Tower on them, they'll sort you out.

Hope & Harlequin

32 Sydney Street (01273) 675222
Mon & Wed-Sat 10.30am-6pm, Tue by appt,
Sun 11am-5pm
www.hopeandharlequin.com

Step into a world of old-time sartorial elegance at this vintage ladies' outfitters, with dresses from the 30s to the 60s and more organza than you can shake a stick at. They also specialise in elegant vintage wedding wear that not only does away with all that bouffant dressed-as-a-cake nonsense but chops the starting price down to a remarkably sensible £200 or so. At that rate you'll only need to save up another £649,800 and you'll have enough for a deposit on a Brighton seafront flat to begin your married life together. Ah, the romance of property speculation.

VINTAGE & RETRO CLOTHING

Dig for Victory

175 Edward Street (01273) 676402
Thurs-Sat 10am-6pm, Mon-Wed by
appointment
digforvictoryclothing.co.uk

There are many vintage shops in Brighton but few feel as authentic as this, a dress shop straight outta the 50s. Choose from off-the-peg tea, prom, wiggle and mod dresses, starting at £110, or select a style you like and have it custom tailored in a fabric of your choosing.

Owner Eleanor has been collecting vintage and reclaimed fabric for years,

FATBOY SLIM'S

all★season fashion tips

Hello! Norman 'Fatboy Slim' Cook here, come to give you some fashion tips! And I reckon I'm a bit of a style guru, because once I was watching Gok's Style Secrets with Zoe and she said: "You should be on this programme, Norman," so she obviously reckons I'd make a better presenter than him! So, without further ado, here's Norm's guide to how to look and feel good, whatever the weather.

Summer

Summers in Brighton always remind me of being a kid. You know – deck chairs, buckets 'n' spades, weeing in the sea. Nowadays I spend my summers idling on the beach, pottering around the house listening to records, or even making my own by cobbling together a few R'n'B samples with a drum loop! No, really! It's as easy as that!!!

And what could be more perfect for those long hot, sticky months than to slip into a cool, thin, colourful, 100% cotton Hawaiian shirt? They're comfortable, stylish, eye-catching, and make you look like a real 'Funk Soul Brother.'

Autumn

Now a lot of people see this time of year as an excuse to start sporting knitwear and favouring such autumnal colours as burnt oranges, dark browns and reds. This I believe is a terrible mistake! You wouldn't catch me going out in a snowstorm dressed all in white!!!

Take a tip from me – dare to be different! Why not go for something colourful, and striking? Like a Hawaiian shirt, say! And, when everyone else is turning up to those Halloween parties in black (yawn!), you'll steal the show with a dazzle of colour on your back!!!

Winter

Like many people I tend to suffer from the winter blues, especially during the long months from January to March. If I look out of my bedroom window in the morning and it's cold, miserable and grey outside, my spirits start to flag and, before I know it, I'm comatose in front of the box with a jazz mag in one hand and a joint in the other, watching Jeremy Kyle harrass absent fathers. God, do I get depressed!! Until, that is, I remember my faithful Hawaiian shirt! Once I've whipped off my jim-jams and got that cool cotton and splash of colour on my back it feels like a little bit of the summer has returned, leaving me with a rosy complexion and a chance again to face the world with a smile. I recommend you do the same. Magic!

Spring

Now during the 'rainy season', a lot of people favour waterproof coats with hoods. This, I believe, is a terrible mistake. And can be extremely dangerous! Did you know that wearing a hood can reduce visibility by up to 37%?!! If, for example, you were crossing the busy A27 between Worthing and Shoreham, your so-called 'sensible' hooded raincoat might protect you from the wet, but would offer precious little protection when you failed to notice the 30-tonne Juggernaught that was hurtling towards you, smashing into you at a 120 miles an hour and crushing your head like a ripe melon.

So don't be silly. Be safe!! Make yourself visible when crossing the road. Why not go out just wearing something brightly-coloured – something like, say, just for the sake of argument… a Hawaiian shirt?!! Sure you might get soaked, catch a cold, or worse, pneumonia, but at least you'll be safe.

Right – I'm off now; I've got until tomorrow to write a new album. Not a problem!!! Praise you!!!!! Norm

Jump the Gun

36 Gardner Street (01273) 626333
Mon-Sat 10am-6pm, Sun 12noon-5pm
www.jumpthegun.co.uk

The UK's only exclusively mod shop, Jump the Gun has been established in Brighton for over twenty years now, and is almost as synonymous with the city as sticks of rock, tattoos and arson. This well-loved store boasts a handsome collection of suits, shirts, parkas, Dr Martens and coats for the dapper gentleman, all at very reasonable prices. The shop's owners are brothers Adam and Jonathan, who live and breathe the mod life – arriving to work on Lambrettas, always dressing smartly and nipping up Little East Street every lunchtime for a bit of how's your father. For those not into the scene, Jump the Gun is still worth a visit, for it is as much about proper tailoring, quality garments, good treatment and looking sharp as it is about mod culture. As

Adam puts it, *"We want our customers to go away looking like a cross between John Steed and Sean Connery"*. Better start cutting down on the pies then...

Immediate Clothing

34 Sydney Street (01273) 603844
Mon-Sat 11am-6pm

If Jump The Gun is The Jam, Immediate Clothing is The Style Council. That's according to new owner, Daren, anyway. Catering for a slightly more sophisticated style than the old Immediate, this is still the best source of vintage menswear in the North Laine. They sell a neat selection of jeans, shirts, jackets and shoes, and when we say neat, we mean neat. Everything in the shop is in meticulous, rainbow order. The house brand includes decent silk paisley shirts and scarves. Prices vary as wildly as your ever changing moods - you can get Levi jeans for as little as £20, or a fancy jacket for a few thousand.

Pretty Eccentric

10 Bond Street (01273) 238342
Mon-Sat 10am-5.30pm, Sun 11am-5pm
www.prettyeccentric.co.uk

Promising traditional looks with a modern twist, this boutique specialises in sumptuous vintage-style dresses and accessories: jewelled flapper dresses, silk kimonos, lace maxis, ostrich feather stoles, art deco necklaces, watch-movement cufflinks. not to mention their trademark steampunk top hats. For those who like a bit of glamour in their wardrobe, this shop will elicit a kid-in-a-candy-store feeling.

Rio

67 Trafalgar Street (01273) 567181
Mon-Sat 11am-6pm

"All about colour" as evidenced by its bright turquoise shop front and array of psychedelic patterned Chenaski shirts. Besides neo-70s menswear, Rio sells an array of Desigual dresses, tops and bags, and Voodoo Vixen retro-print dresses. They also stock some rather sexy boots that are ideal for the vampire goth in your life. For those who want vintage style without that musty smell.

Shabitat

Lewes Road, opposite The Bear pub
(01273) 677577
Mon-Fri 9am-5pm, Sat-Sun 11am-5pm
www.magpie.coop/shabitat
www.leftover.co.uk

A dirty great sky-blue warehouse by the Vogue Gyratory might not be most people's first port of call for intriguing second-hand clobber, but the selection in the back room of Magpie Recycling Co-op's HQ is so mind-bendingly cheap you'd be well advised to drop by before you hit North Laine and lash out a fortune on a garish orange tie with an inexplicable stain. Coats are £3, trousers two, and if you've only got a quid you can still get some headgear. There's also a smattering of 'reconstructed' garments by Leftover, giving a new lease of life to sweatshirts and skirts via the clothcutter's equivalent of gene splicing.

The remainder of this cavernous barn is given over to second-hand furniture, the pricing strategy for which eludes us, ranging as it does from £2 for a table to a bizarre painting of Hattie Jacques' disembodied head floating on 60s wallpaper for £200.

HIGH STREET & DESIGNER LABELS

For the ladies there's a wide range of clothes and shoe shops around the Old Lanes including the likes of Design Lab, Mottoo (for Paul Smith and Nicole Farhi) and Morgan in Duke Street; French Connection, Jigsaw, All Saints, Monsoon and Coast on East Street; Moist, Ted Baker, Ghost and Oasis in Duke's Lane. If you're looking for Miss Selfridge, H&M and Warehouse you'll find them in Churchill Square, along with most other predictable high street retailers.

Guys, err... Topman and H&M anyone?

Second-hand Clothing

In James Joyce's Ulysses, Bloom famously hypothesised that it would be near impossible to cross Dublin without passing a pub. Brighton's equivalent would be second-hand clothing shops, of which there are many. Here's the Cheeky Guide's top 5 picks, to help you navigate your own vintage odyssey.

Dirty Harry: Sydney Street. Easy to spot with its iconic painted shopfront. Three floors of men's and women's. Good selection of basics, with some interesting pieces.

Beyond Retro: Vine Street. HUGE warehouse full of men's and women's… everything. The department store of vintage clothes shops.

Kate & Aud: Trafalgar Street. Lots of pretty, frilly, lacy bits. Can be pricy but also has lots of sale bins with 3 for £10 offers.

To Be Worn Again: Sydney Street and Kensington Gardens. Two stores worth of vintage gear for boys 'n gals, shoes, bags and accessories.

Oxfam: North Street. Honestly, most charity shops in Brighton are worth a look-in but this Oxfam in particular has a well-ordered range of good quality clothes. Also includes handmade/reworked pieces by volunteers.

Sunglasses not included

MUSICAL INSTRUMENTS

Adaptatrap Percussion
26 Trafalgar Street (01273) 672722
Mon-Sat 10.30am-6pm
adaptatrap.co.uk

Brighton's own world music and drum emporium is still as exotic and atmospheric as ever. Since the advent of the smoking ban owner Les has been unable to display his incredible talent for being able to restring a sitar whilst smoking an entire roll-up without taking it out of his mouth. He can still, however, offer advice on a myriad of melodic and percussive requirements while simultaneously putting the world to rights. Other than their excellent range of selected hand drums from everywhere imaginable, you'll find balafons, berimbaus, gongs and cutting-edge koras (made by the man himself); singing bowls, harmonicas, wood-block frogs and thumb pianos; and for those hard-core loved ones who truly have everything, why not plump for a wooden nose whistle? You can try it all, and the quirky but open-hearted Adaptatrap crew are always available to offer their expertise and counsel. Plenty of info about gigs, workshops and shamanic weekends, as well as teachers for those newly acquired instruments.

The Guitar, Amp and Keyboard Centre
66 & 78 North Road (01273) 665400
Mon-Sat 9.30am-5.30pm, Sun 11am-4pm
www.gak.co.uk

Created from the barrow-boy charm of its haggle-friendly owner Gary, who turned up in Brighton twenty years ago with just a broken banjo and the gift of the gab. Since then he

UNDERSTATED CLOTHING

Passport
108 St James's Street (01273) 621422
Mon-Fri 10.30am-4.30pm, Sat 10am-5pm
www.passportmenswear.com

Many's the time we've walked past this place and thought "Ow! Jesus! My eyes...I'm blind!" for it has to be said that owner Raj is not afraid of a little colour. From the bright pink silky suit in the window to the dazzling array of lurid shirts, waistcoats and ties that hang inside, this is a walk-in-wardrobe for exhibitionists and anyone considering a career in stand up comedy. It's not just startling shades; there's plenty of paisley on offer as well as some more vertigo-inducing patterns. Be on your guard though – on our last visit Raj said cheerfully, *"I've got a new delivery coming soon that will be even more colourful!"*

WE DO GUITAR REPAIRS!
All work undertaken, even this!
ASK INSIDE FOR DETAILS....

has built himself an empire which seems to dominate half of North Road, with separate shops for every imaginable instrument. There's the Drum Cavern, Bass Basement, Didge Depot, Bongo Boutique and Mouth Organ Mezzanine to name but a few. True, GAK has become a victim of its own success, growing so large that the intimacy between customer and seller has been lost, but, despite that, still seems to have kept some of Gary's "sod it, call it a tenner, mate" approach to life. Will accept body parts as down payment.

BURST BANANA
SLIGHTLY BRUISED
RELUCTANT SALE
£1

Mudpie Music Ltd
17 Trafalgar Street (01273) 606335
Mon-Sat 10.30am-6pm
mudpiemusicltd.com

"Working in a mainstream music store is like saying you love food but work in Tesco. Well this is a deli." Specialising in pre-owned and vintage guitars and basses, plus amps and accessories, Mudpie Music is run by local guitarist Alfie (*"Here's something 'cheeky' for you: me and my customers all suffer from GAS. Guitar Acquisition Syndrome"*) who delivers a friendly and informative customer service. He emphasises that it's about getting the right guitar for you, not about trends or brand names - though he does stock vintage Gibson, Gretsch, Rickenbacker and Hofner. Look out at local gigs for Alfie, who says that he loves bumping into his customers (*"so they know I can't cheat them!"*)

FLEA / MARKETS

Brighton Flea Market

31a Upper St James's Street
(01273) 624006
Mon-Fri 10am-5pm, Sat-Sun 10.30am-5pm
flea-markets.co.uk

Keep going up St James's Street and you'll find this bright pink, two-storey building just after the road bends. Compared with Snoopers it's slim pickings: there's little in the way of clothes, way too many shelves of old video cassettes and a paucity of good furniture. But unlike Snoopers, you're more likely to find a bargain or two here: prices are much more realistic and those who relish quirky old ornaments can pick up a pair of eyeless carved gazelles. Fans of horrifically bad taxidermy are also well served; how about a wall mountable head of someone's pet dog, or a squirrel dressed as a dentist? Someone here clearly has a sense of humour; it's almost worth visiting just for the signs and the occasionally hilarious window display. If only the alligator lamp was for sale.

North Laine Antique & Flea Market

5 Upper Gardner Street (01273) 600894
Mon-Sat 10am-5.30pm, Sun 10am-4pm

This place has the odd absurdly priced item but in general the mark-ups are less eye watering than you grow to expect in Brighton. Clamber up to the roof space and there's a rather nifty corner of musical instruments, including a bunch of 80s keyboards for around a tenner each, perfect for recreating those cheesy monochrome pop videos, which we always assumed were socio-political commentary on the Thatcher years, but on reflection, were just pretentious rubbish.

The Open Market

Marshalls Row (01273) 695728
Mon-Fri 9am-5pm, Sat-Sun 10am-5pm
brightonopenmarket.co.uk

Newly rebuilt with a sign that is a work of art in itself, the Open Market lies just off the London Road and houses a treasure trove of independent retailers. From apothecaries to artpothecaries, pet stores to patisseries, there's a little of everything here, with plenty of room still for the traditional meat, fish and greengrocer businesses that have been here for eons. Visit Shaboutique and the Eco Makers Emporium for upcycled furniture and clothing, browse the second-hand book and record stalls, or sample Croatian wines at the Croatian wine shop.

Alongside the regular Saturday market there are often other events taking place - live music, dance, circus performance, visiting guest markets. Our favourites have to be a large 4-lane Scalextric racing track for young and old alike, and a children's day featuring Derek the Dolphin who proves that dolphins really are the cleverest mammals around as he takes on all comers on a giant Connect 4.

Snoopers Paradise

7-8 Kensington Gardens (01273) 602558
Mon-Sat 10am-6pm, Sun 11am-4pm

Brighton's largest indoor flea market, with two floors of stock covering everything from 70s plastic furniture to toys you'd forgotten you once owned. Snoopers really is a cherished Brighton institution; somewhere to while away an afternoon getting lost in the maze of stalls and perusing such marvels as Victorian ephemera and second-hand undies. And for lovers of antique and retro clothes there are some good rails to be found in the back on the right. However, if you have a heart condition, you might wish to keep away as you could find yourself taking the lord's name in vain while uttering things like, *"Sixty quid... for that?!"* or, *"I threw one of those away last year and they're selling it here for £200! Aaaaarggghhh!!!"*

Then take a deep breath and thank the lord that Snoopers hasn't yet been turned into a café bar or luxury housing. Amen.

Upper Gardner Street Market

Saturdays only, 8am-5pm

This small weekly outdoor market in North Laine has been going since Bruce Forsyth first wore flares. We must admit, we've never found a bargain here but know friends who swear by it. But then perhaps this world can be divided into those who come away from a jumble sale with a mint-condition original Moog synthesiser for £3 and those who end up just buying a pot plant. But we digress, get here early and you might pick up a cool pair of jeans, an old typewriter or a good book for a few quid. Arrive after noon and it'll be you and a hundred other people all huddled round a broken cine camera that's going for £60. But, quality aside, it's pleasant to wander down and peruse the junk, and a good alternative to being squashed in Kensington Gardens on a hot, busy Saturday afternoon.

Where to Sit on

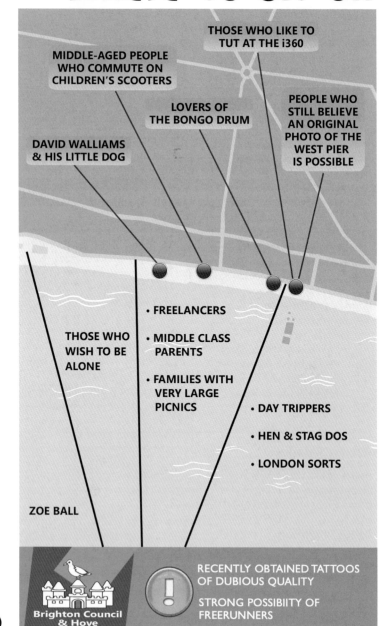

THOSE WHO LIKE TO
TUT AT THE i360

MIDDLE-AGED PEOPLE
WHO COMMUTE ON
CHILDREN'S SCOOTERS

LOVERS OF
THE BONGO DRUM

PEOPLE WHO
STILL BELIEVE
AN ORIGINAL
PHOTO OF THE
WEST PIER
IS POSSIBLE

DAVID WALLIAMS
& HIS LITTLE DOG

THOSE WHO
WISH TO BE
ALONE

- FREELANCERS

- MIDDLE CLASS
  PARENTS

- FAMILIES WITH
  VERY LARGE
  PICNICS

- DAY TRIPPERS

- HEN & STAG DOS

- LONDON SORTS

ZOE BALL

RECENTLY OBTAINED TATTOOS
OF DUBIOUS QUALITY

STRONG POSSIBIITY OF
FREERUNNERS

Brighton Council
& Hove

Brighton Beach

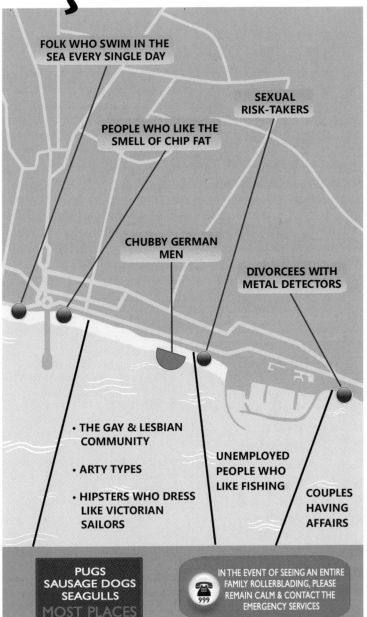

FOLK WHO SWIM IN THE
SEA EVERY SINGLE DAY

SEXUAL
RISK-TAKERS

PEOPLE WHO LIKE THE
SMELL OF CHIP FAT

CHUBBY GERMAN
MEN

DIVORCEES WITH
METAL DETECTORS

- THE GAY & LESBIAN
  COMMUNITY

- ARTY TYPES

- HIPSTERS WHO DRESS
  LIKE VICTORIAN
  SAILORS

UNEMPLOYED
PEOPLE WHO
LIKE FISHING

COUPLES
HAVING
AFFAIRS

PUGS
SAUSAGE DOGS
SEAGULLS
MOST PLACES

IN THE EVENT OF SEEING AN ENTIRE
FAMILY ROLLERBLADING, PLEASE
REMAIN CALM & CONTACT THE
EMERGENCY SERVICES

999

Tearooms & Cafés

KEY TO CAFÉ LOCATIONS

C	– **City centre**
H	– **Hove**
HA	– **Hanover**
K	– **Kemptown**
NL	– **North Laine**
OL	– **Old Lanes**
PC	– **Preston Circus**
S	– **Seafront**
SD	– **Seven Dials**
SW	– **Brighton Sewers**

Bill's (NL)

100 North Street (01273) 692894
Mon-Sat 8am-11pm, Sun 9am-10.30pm
bills-website.co.uk

A surprising but welcome export from the nearby *Wicker Man* island of Lewes, Bill's initially seemed like a vision of the future for cafés the world over, overshadowing much that once seemed fresh and innovative in Brighton. Alas, gone is the fruit and vegetable shop element of the business, along with much of the other produce that used to line every spare bit of wall space. A more modest selection of Bill's own brand sauces and biscuits and the giant bunches of red chillis that hang from the ceiling are all that remain of the formerly overwhelming sensory spectacle in this vast single room. However, be not downhearted, for the food, which is after all the main event, is still a visual and taste sensation. Out go the more obvious quiches, pizzas and fishfinger sandwiches, and in come more varied items such as crispy lemon squid, pork chops and roast salmon - there are still some salads but the menu now leans more towards restaurant style fare, though the breakfasts (served till 4pm, yes the world is a confusing place) remain intact and are, while not the cheapest, among the most enticing in town. Or how about a lemon meringue cheesecake in a glass - a pudding in a drink?

Despite being located in Brighton's draughty old bus depot (hence the huge ceiling), Bill's thrives in winter and, should you feel a bit of a gust round your gusset, you'll find the staff whizzing around handing out hot-water bottles on especially cold days – another nice touch. .

In a phenomenal local success story, Bill's has now been franchised to about 70 outlets all over the country, but we think ours is still one of the best. Recommended.

Blackbird Tea Rooms (OL)

30 Ship Street   (01273) 249454
Daily 8.30am-5.30pm
blackbirdtearooms.com

An Edwardian-style English tea room with a Farrow & Ball paint job in the heart of the Old Lanes. Service is provided by a team of lovely young ladies in traditional white pinafores who, should you bring along old Uncle Bert, may have him tugging at his collar and reaching for the heart pills. As with the decor, the food is a mix of traditional (eggs benedict or boiled egg and soldiers) and modern (granola, sour dough) with the odd speciality such as Blackbird rarebit. Sad to report the blackbird part of the rarebit is actually portobello mushrooms, but tasty nonetheless. All food is of a high standard, there are two floors, lots of lovely old tins and jars to look at on the shelves, attentive service and occasional breakfast deals on their website. Perfect for bringing the family, taking a date or visiting on your own, where you can sit by the window eating cream tea and twirling your 'tache.

Choccywoccydoodah Café (OL)

3 Meeting House Lane   (01273) 329462
Mon-Sat 10am-6pm, Sun 11am-5pm
www.choccywoccydoodah.com

Unique, sensual and camp as Christmas, this is the café you'd expect to find in heaven, where it's perfectly OK to have hot chocolate for starters, truffles for main course and chocolate cake for dessert, and no one gives a fig about their waistband. And it is, of course, exceptionally good; the hot chocolate is made from just pure melted Belgian chocolate and milk and is so thick you could float an egg on the top.

Located above the newly relocated Choccywoccydoodahdogband shop, you'd have to be colour blind not to be dazzled by the elegance of the place. The windows and interior are full of chocolate figurines, skulls and extravagant cakes decorated by chief chocolate sculptor Dave Pop, and there's even their private Empire Room that can be hired for events where the price includes all the drinks, chocolate and cake you can keep down in two hours, most frequently hen parties pigging out before wobbling off to strike fear into young single men on the seafront.

An orgy of chocolate, friendly service and a discreet trouser-widening service round the back.

The Dorset Street Bar (NL)

28 North Road (01273) 605423
Mon-Sat 10am-11pm, Sun 10am-8pm
www.thedorset.co.uk

A visit to Brighton is not complete without a coffee and a pose outside the Dorset. As well as offering a range of beers, warm drinks and slightly Frenchified food, the Dorset has an enviable location on the corner of North Road and Gardner Street where, on warm summer afternoons, you can sit outside and marvel at the style gurus parading through North Laine. Sadly, food and service quality

have taken a dive in recent years, not helped by their expansion into the old Capers café premises next door - the staff seem overstretched and under-interested and the room ambience doesn't seem to work when scaled up. Stick to the old pub bit on the corner, and watch out for the vibrating table by the back wall - if the dishwasher is on you'll feel it through the floorboards.

The Flour Pot Bakery (NL/HA)

36 Sydney Street (01273) 621942
124 Elm Grove. (01273) 625854
Mon-Sat 8am-7pm, Sun 9am-6pm,
at Elm Grove closing *"follows the sunset"*
flour-pot.co.uk

These newish local bakery kids on the block have moved beyond pure wholesale to open a couple of cool, simply designed shop-cum-cafés that flog a fantastic range of their artisanal breads and own savoury and sweet snack products. Outdoor seating is a special feature of both establishments; at Sydney Street you can perch on the pavement under the trees and Elm Grove has a purpose-built front terrace for basking in the sun (though you may have to shout occasionally to be heard above the traffic or the kids practising their hip hop routines at the school over the road). Coffee comes from that other burgeoning local business Small Batch, who seem to be supplying most of Brighton's caffeine intake at the moment, and the quality and imagination that goes into stuff like their breakfast buns and flatbreads (which must be the flattest flatbreads made this side of Cairo) means the Flour Pot may soon be supplying most of your carbohydrate intake. Pretty much impossible to resist.

Guarana Bar (NL)

36 Sydney Street (01273) 600557
Mon-Sat 10am-6pm, Sun 12noon-5pm
www.guaranaco.com

Guarana is not, as many mistakenly
assume when they see the sign on
this odd café-cum-shop, the product
of seabirds' bottoms, but rather a
South American plant that makes
a 'super-charged' natural energy
drink, said to put a skip in your step
and hairs on your chest. And very
refreshing it is too, provided you like
the taste of wet grass. It is, however,
just one of the many unusual and
natural stimulating drinks and herbs
on offer here, like wheatgrass,
spirulina, acai and bee pollen (ok, that
last one wasn't a drink OR a herb.
Is it an insect scraping?), along with
their nutritional supplements and
aphrodisiacs. Ideal for those in search
of a healthy pick-me-up.

Infinity Foods Kitchen (NL)

50 Gardner Street (01273) 670743
Mon-Sat 9am-5pm, Sun 10am-4pm
infinityfoodskitchen.co.uk

This veggie/vegan café in the heart of
North Laine was born out of Infinity
Foods' incredible success and has
the food to match. The menu is 95%
organic, the coffee is fair trade, they
offer a takeaway option, and there's
thorough information on which items
support your current intolerance, be
it dairy, wheat, gluten or myxomatosis.
Expect queuing at lunchtime, though
you should always be able to find a seat
upstairs and, besides, those salads are
well worth waiting for – you can almost
feel your body quiver with gratitude as
you shovel them down.

Iydea (NL)

17 Kensington Gardens (01273) 667992
(See Veggie Food chapter)

Jack and Linda Mills' Traditional Fish Smokers (S)

197 Kings Road Arches (01273) 723064
Open daily

Located just to the left of the Fishing Museum, this is the place to stop for a seafood snack on Brighton seafront. Ex-fisherman and fisherwoman Jack and Linda have now been here for more over a decade smoking kippers and the like in their tiny black smokehouse on one side of the boardwalk, and on the other side dishing out their mouth-wateringly delicious fish soup, smoked mackerel, crab sandwiches and other delicacies of the sea. Seating is provided in the open air courtesy of upturned boats or the low wall opposite the arches, so if it's raining don't expect to find sanctuary from the weather while you slurp on your soup. On a recent visit Jack insisted to us that he won't be retiring until he's carried out of the place in a box. A woman in the queue quipped, "*Smoked?*"

Marwood (OL)

52 Ship Street (01273) 382063
Sun-Wed 8am-8pm, Thur-Sat 8am-11pm
themarwood.com

While coffee houses and bars have, of late, played the hipster card with jam jars for cups, paving slabs for plates and twigs for cutlery, Marwood – and its brother Presuming Ed – appear to be the creation of a singular (and slightly unhinged) mind. Decorated with a random assortment of tat, toys, Star Wars cardboard cutouts, mannequin limbs and torsos, coming here is rather like stepping into the set for a Punchdrunk show themed around The Banana Splits. Look up from your coffee and you'll notice things like a space hopper suspended from the ceiling like a hot air balloon, underneath of which Sooty, Sweep and Soo hang out in a basket. True, the furniture has calmed down of late – you're less likely to be sitting at a table made of doors and a chair that's a pile of lampshades – but upstairs next to the Uncle Monty style parlour there's now a room whose furniture appears to be 90s Apple Macs nailed to scaffolding planks.

This is though more than just a coffee house. Sure, the cake is excellent and the service suitably mañana but it's also a hub of creativity. There are life drawing classes, midweek talks and other events usually listed on the notice board by the counter. And while they do have signs like *'Hey you with the laptop, drink more coffee!'* we think they secretly like the fact the place attracts folk planning to make a film, start an indie magazine or plotting to bring down the government. And why 'Marwood'? We'll leave it to the *Withnail and I* fans to figure it out. Highly recommended.

The Meeting Place (S)

Hove Sea Wall, Kingsway, right on the seafront! (01273) 206417
7am to sunset all year round (weather permitting)
themeetingplacecafe.co.uk

Set up as a temporary kiosk in 1935, the council characteristically dragged its heels in allowing planning permission for this seafront café as a more permanent structure and the thumbs-up only came through in 2002. Not one to miss an opportunity, its owner soon had the place rebuilt… five metres to the left, thus craftily relocating from Hove to Brighton (well who wouldn't, given the choice?)

The Meeting Place ranks among the ten best reasons for living in Brighton: it's literally a stone's throw from the sea, the views are terrific and, on a warm summer morning, it's the perfect spot to have breakfast, read the paper in your pants, get a suntan and jump in the sea afterwards. Heroically it stays open throughout the bleakest of winters but as it's a Brighton tradition to make a pilgrimage here on Christmas morning for a coffee, you'll even see queues then. Those with a refined palate be warned, this is standard caff grub – jacket potatoes, toasties, chips and cakes, but it's still the café to come to if you want the traditional Brighton seafront experience rather than the designer one.

Metrodeco Tea Salon (K)

38 Upper St James's Street (01273) 677243
Sun-Thurs 9.30am-6pm, Fri-Sat 9.30am-8pm
www.metro-deco.com

Leave the 21st century behind and enter an elegant 1930s themed tea room, complete with leopardskin covered chairs, chandeliers, ornate mirrors and a huge range of teas including alcoholic tea cocktails. Choose from green, white, black, red, a rose-coloured one called Pink Pride or our favourite, Yellow Polka Dot, which comes complete with a musical bikini-shaped biscuit. Downstairs they've also got a lovely vintage themed space available for hire. The perfect antidote to the modern coffee shop and what Larry David referred to as 'those vanilla bullshit latte things.'

The Mock Turtle (OL)

4 Pool Valley (01273) 327380
Daily 9am-6pm

With its paper doilies, tablecloths, brass-dolphin door knocker, jugs and plates on the walls, this tea shop revels in being utterly unhip, though for many these elements are precisely what makes it so endearing. Cherished for its dazzling selection of traditional cakes, omelettes, pork sausages, homemade jams, its own range of teas and legendary doughnuts, it's no surprise The Times once included it in the top 50 teashops of Britain. Our friend Paul loves it so much he was inspired to write a poem about it, which he's learned off by heart and will happily recite to you should you spot him in here (look for a man with a dreamy look in his eyes, covered in crumbs.)

For those of a competitive nature, to eat a whole one of their cannonball-sized doughnuts is challenge enough, but if you manage it without getting sugar all over your nose and chin you deserve to be rewarded with a large slice of their lemon cake.

Pavilion Gardens Café (NL)

Off New Road behind a hedge
Mar-Oct 8am-6pm *"when it's nice weather"*
www.paviliongardenscafe.co.uk

The only café in the centre of Brighton where you can enjoy a cuppa accompanied by the gentle rustling of trees (though you may have to fight off persistent pigeons). This Brighton institution commands a splendid view of the Royal Pavilion from its position at the edge of the gardens and is a perfect escape from the traffic and shopping hordes just yards away. Run by the same family since the kiosk was built in 1941 and still baking their famous rock cakes on the premises, practically the only things that have changed over the decades are the plastic furniture and the fact that you no longer need to be wearing a hat to get served. The café and surrounding gardens also have the rare distinction of being a space shared equally by that threatened species the Brighton bongo player and crusty old colonels in cravats and straw boaters, making it a special place for people watching as well as hanging out with a Ribena and nut slice.

Presuming Ed (L)

114 London Road. (01273) 911991
Mon-Sat 8am-7pm, Sun 9am-7pm
www.presuming-ed.com

Employing the same eccentric rag and bone man aesthetic as companion café, Marwood, Presuming Ed took a much-despised bank and turned it into a groovy hangout, moulded from paperback books; they serve as wallpaper, scary sculpture material, tables, chairs and even parts of the counter are made of them.

It's mostly (good) coffee, cake and toasted sandwiches, so don't expect a fry-up, but do explore their junk-tastic secret garden out the back, where those nostalgic for the old Two Way bookshop in North Laine will discover what happened to their sign (and presumably, all their books).

In the on-going gentrification of the London Road area, this is one of the highlights. And as with Marwood, you'll need to ask the Withnail fans where the name comes from.

Rock-Ola Coffee Bar (NL)

29 Tidy Street (01273) 673744
Mon-Fri 10.30am-4.30pm, Sat 9.30am-4.30pm
rockolacoffeebar.com

Operating as an adjunct to The Wax Factor record shop round the corner on Trafalgar Street and run by Alan Wax's missus, the Rock-Ola takes a hefty stab at recreating the feeling that Tommy Steele (ask your dad) might be about to wander in off the street and strum a few chords while playing bongos with his quiff. The chromed-up furniture, US sparkly plastic seating, novelty cruet sets, posters and memorabilia all goose up the 50s/early-60s feel, while much of the food echoes a simpler gastronomic era with dishes such as corned-beef hash, shepherd's pie and apple-and-blackberry crumble. Best of all, there's the ancient jukebox from which the place takes its name, stacked with period 45s and totally free – ideal for playing Crispian St Peters' The Pied Piper eighteen times in succession (though the staff will lob a Betty Boop salt shaker at your noggin if you do).

MY BRIGHTON & HOVE

Name: BRIAN SATCHEL
local playwright

1. The Whistling Teapot Where else in Brighton could you order bacon and cabbage soup and still have change from 50p? And they show old Laurel and Hardy films in the afternoon. And they still allow you to smoke. Marvellous. Mind you, it did close down in 1978.

2. Shabby's Tweed Emporium The place to buy your second-hand slacks. The gent who runs it is a lovely fellow and often has an old German Shepherd, Bob. He's a nice fellow too. Boom boom! But seriously folks, where else in Brighton could you buy a porkpie hat for under a quid? And they let you smoke. Pity it closed over twenty years ago.

3. Arthur Grumble's Tobacco and Snuff Shop God bless Arthur Grumble. The most cantankerous misanthropic man I have ever met! But he certainly gives a good shag. Boom boom! But seriously, you'll not find a finer purveyor of tobacco this side of the planet. And it's actually still open! Pity I stopped smoking five years ago but then, as the missus keeps reminding me, it is for the good of me health. And besides…. oh eck she's returned. Blast! Better sign off. If she catches me with this pie in me hand she'll, ow, ouch, aagghhh…

Kitchen utensil mobile courtesy of Treacle and Co.

(it often seems disappointingly empty), letting your gaze wander from the Cliff Richard plate clock to pictures of Bet Lynch and the Charles Spencer quote on the side of the pianola.

The food is all home-made; choose from cream teas, cakes, scones and finger sandwiches or one of their special sandwich meals with names like Balmoral, Buckingham or Victoria. Previous owners David and James used to serve what they claimed was the lengthiest-titled meal in the world. It's worth asking for even though they've stopped doing it: the Lady Diana Spencer, Princes of Wales, Queen of Hearts, 10 Year Anniversary, Your Death Has Torn Our Lives Apart, Farewell Dear Princess Queen of Hearts, Forever in Our Thoughts, Memorial Afternoon Tea!

The Tea Cosy Tea Rooms (K)

3 George Street (01273) 677055
Wed-Fri 12pm-5pm Sat 12pm-5.30pm
theteacosy.co.uk

A reminder that Brighton does eccentricity better than anywhere else in the UK, this royalty-obsessed teahouse harps back to the days of sugar tongs, china teacups, standing up for the National anthem on a Sunday and lifting the pinkie when slurping your tea. The whole place is decked out magnificently with Charles and Di memorabilia, flags, signed photos of Dot Cotton, a pianola with a mind of its own, paintings of the royal family and a bizarre cabinet of knitted creatures. You could easily spend an afternoon here on your own

Treacle and Co (H)

164 Church Road (01273) 933695
Mon-Fri 8.30am-5.30pm, Sat 9am-5.30pm,
Sun 10am-5pm
treacleandco.co.uk

Formerly a butchers, Treacle is a café in the heart of Hove that boils its own jam, writes its menus on an old rolling school black board and is decorated with kitchen utensil mobiles, entomological curios, bird prints and antlers. Best-loved for its cakes, it's a popular afternoon spot for Hove mums getting high on gingerbread lattes, detox juices and salted caramel tarts. At lunchtime it can get busy; best to get there early if you're after a sit-down meal of banana bread and bacon butties, but don't arrive too early; they only serve hot food after 12pm. A few more places like this on the map and we might have to start taking Hove more seriously.

LORD DEVANEY'S PERCOLATIONS

Like T.S. Eliot's Prufrock, I have measured out my life in coffee spoons. And birthdays. But mostly coffee spoons. From dubious dips into jars of low-priced instacaf, through the portioning of acrid powder into discoloured paper funnels and the 80s drip drip drip of filter-filled pot, all the way to the milky stirrings of a latte revolution, I have seen coffee grow from an exotic treat to a daily necessity.

As in the rest of the country, shops belonging to corporations with curious taxation arrangements have sprung up across Brighton and Hove, often gathering like buses in pairs or threes down major thoroughfares, to sate this newfound thirst for the bean. In their shadow a vast number of smaller, more independent, operators have risen, each with their own unique atmosphere. No longer is the art of "proper" coffee-making a secret practice known only to those with access to a steamy Gaggia and a Mediterranean accent. Nowadays – to misquote the legal profession – it seems like everyone's a barista.

So which to choose? After weeks of hard-wrought research, sleepless nights and palpitations, here are the results from the Devaney jury.

GOLD: TAYLOR ST BARISTAS

28 Queens Road
taylor-st.com

As the name suggests, this is somewhere that takes pride in its coffee, and in how it brews it. Taylor Street wears its expertise lightly, like a rocket scientist talking ping pong. Confusingly situated in Queens Road (the name is a reference to the founders' antipodean roots rather than a glitch in planning permission), this is a little bit of Australia on the south coast of England. Designed more for the discerning office worker than the overt hipster, Taylor Street is still the coffee connoisseur's central city stop of choice, and in addition it must be noted that their range of teas and chai would do any lover of the cuppa proud.

SILVER: MARWOOD

(see entry earlier in chapter)

BRONZE: RED ROASTER

1d St James's Street
Mon-Sat 7am-7pm, Sun 8am-6.30pm
redroaster.co.uk

Here the beans are actually roasted before your very nostrils, with a wide variety of roasts available, not just to drink on site but to take home and fix for yourself. The open plan approach allows you to see the café at work, with the staff swapping between kitchen, counter and roaster like cheerfully-deranged ants. As much a part of the community as a coffee house, Red Roaster often plays host to live events – music, poetry readings, plays, etc – and even offers a coffee beer.

HONOURABLE MENTIONS:

SMALL BATCH COFFEE (various): So good, it's become a mini franchise all over town. Not just for their coffee, but also for the Flour Pot Bakery sausage rolls.

PRESUMING ED (London Road): The new kid on the block. It's like someone raided a 1970s branch of WH Smiths and added caffeine.

COFFEE@33 (Trafalgar Street): Presuming Ed in twenty years' time. Quality coffee and excellent cookie dough that you can bake yourself.

Veggie Food

VEGGIE SHOPS

Infinity Foods

25 North Road (01273) 603563
Mon-Sat 9.30am-6pm, Sun 11am-5pm
www.infinityfoods.co.uk

Brighton's much-loved health food shop stocks everything your (healthy) heart desires. Yogi teas, organic turnips, grains, nuts, seeds and tofu burgers all under one roof, and organic bread baked on the premises. Whether you're a veggie, a vegan or allergic to yak hair, you'll find something here to suit your palate. Also handy for its notice board if you're looking to share a room with a cat-owning, non-smoking vegetarian or need a lift to Belgium. Infinity is a co-op too, so you can even feel saintly about shopping here.

Vegetarian Shoes

12 Gardner Street (01273) 685685
Mon-Sat 10am-6pm, Wed 1pm-6pm
www.vegetarian-shoes.co.uk

Yes, very funny, we know you don't eat shoes (unless you're Charlie Chaplin). This shop sells leather-free shoes in various styles, from Doc Martens to Birkenstocks. They've also got trainers made from hemp, so we guess you could smoke 'em if you were desperate.

The Prince George

5 Trafalgar Street (01273) 681055
Food served Mon-Sat 12noon-9pm,
Sun 12noon *"till we run out and then there's
light snacks"*
princegeorge.pub

Sunday lunch at the Prince George
is a blessing for any vegetarian, with
not a bleeding carcass in sight. Instead,
punters indulge in sweet potato
wellingtons and flat mushroom and
cheddar nut roasts for under a tenner.
In the week, whether it's street food
or a big-old pub lunch, the menu
offers generous portions of food for
around £9: beer-battered halloumi
and chips, falafel burgers or a selection
of meat-free Mexican favourites. Such
is the food quality, even carnivorous
types have been known to eat here,
although they are given a pat-down
at the door in case they're trying to
smuggle in the odd chicken leg.

Iydea

17 Kensington Gardens (01273) 667992
Mon-Sun 9.30am-5.30pm
105 Western Road (01273) 965904
Mon-Sat 9.30am-10pm, Sun 9.30am-5.30pm
www.iydea.co.uk

Fast food for vegetarians who abhor
chips and ketchup, this cosy café has
quality main courses such as casseroles,
enchiladas and their slightly alarming
brie-stuffed veggie balls, over which
you get to throw as many salads and
cooked veg as you can carry. For a
refreshing change the prices (£5ish to
less than £8) actually reflect the cost
of vegetables and the food is tasty
enough to get even your carnivorous
mates smacking their lips. The place
also inadvertently functions as a kind
of veggie dating agency as it's not
uncommon to end up sharing a
table with strangers but, if you don't
fancy squashing in amongst hungry
Brightonians, their branch on Western
Road offers considerably more
elbow room.

Typical vegetarian on his mobile

Wai Kika Moo Kau

11a Kensington Gardens (01273) 671117
Mon-Thur 9am-6pm, Fri-Sat 9am-9.30pm,
Sun 9.30am-6pm
waikikamookau.co.uk

After some ill-advised flirting with a meat as well as veggie menu a few years ago, which did rather make a nonsense of the name (translated phonetically as 'why kick a moo cow.'), this is back on the straight and narrow with a heavily vegan-slanted selection of breakfasts, assorted international versions of the humble sandwich, and that old warhorse the veggie burger. As carnivores we find the chocolate and avocado mousse rather, um, challenging, but this place is a godsend for vegans, who in most towns are made to stand on the pavement chewing a lolly stick while their friends sit in the warm laughing and throwing fried eggs at each other.

We Love Falafel

37 Sydney Street (01273) 604206
Mon-Sat 11am-6pm
welovefalafel.co.uk

During the past couple of years, falafels have become something of a fashion item in Brighton: not only do plenty of lunch-style spots sell them but people are even wearing them as earrings. We Love Falafel serves one of the top chickpea lunches, and adds a new spin with its sweet potato or beetroot falafel for those wanting to eat 'outside the box'. The shop itself is basically just a kitchen with a small countertop and whether you want your falafel wrapped, grilled, spicy or in a salad, everything comes to about a fiver – perfect for a quick bite on the go.

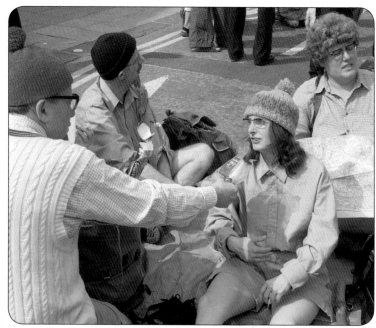

Typical vegetarian family on holiday

VEGETARIAN BRIGHTON

by Joseph Nixon

If you're a vegetarian, a vegan or even a fruitarian, one of the best things about Brighton is that it's possible to live an animal-product-free existence with great ease here. Unlike certain towns in this country, which will remain nameless (although Mansfield comes pretty close), you won't be met with a look of blank incomprehension if you request a veggie sausage in a café nor burnt at the stake for witchcraft, effeminacy and general oddness if you enquire about the possibility of a nut roast in your local

A typical vegetarian

("*Aye, we'll be having a nut roast tonight alright. Fetch the flaming torches, Bert*"). So veggie-friendly is Brighton that I've seen clueless meat-eaters who request roast beef being turned away from vegetarian pubs with a cry of "*Sorry mate, we don't do that sort of thing in here*".

To anyone who, like me, spent his or her teenage years subsisting on a diet of burger-bar 'vegetarian specials' (a roll and salad, without the burger) or the ubiquitous restaurant veggie dish of the day (always, always bloody lasagne or some bland pasta dish), this city is a godsend. It's great living in a place with so many veggie-only eateries, where for once you'll be free of the paranoia (which secretly affects all vegetarians) that you'll accidentally be served a meat dish which you'll consume with relish while saying, "*Bloody hell, these sausages are good. Almost like the real thing*".

The best thing about Brighton veggie grub is that the eateries don't conform to the 'vegetarian food must be worthy, earnest, bland, look like a beige cowpat and taste like the contents of a lawnmower' rule. Some of the stuff on offer in Brighton looks and tastes so good that even your hardened carnivore mates might be tempted.

Typical fruitarian restaurant

VEGGIE RESTAURANTS

Planet India

4 Richmond Parade (01273) 818149
Tues-Sat 6pm-10pm and 'some Sundays'

Despite the existence of 200 million vegetarians in India, precious few have been inclined to nip over to Brighton to open a restaurant. It took a man from Luton to redress that balance with a meatless menu and a singular vision for decor: Planet India doesn't really resemble any Indian restaurant you've been to before. Along with the mismatched furnishings, pale pink walls and a floor that looks like a recycled pub carpet, you'll find reggae playing softly in the background and the bust of Bob Marley casually smoking in the corner. Service here is friendly, prompt and, if it's the owner, barefoot.

There are veggie and vegan curries (with most dishes being gluten-free)

and the Dhai bhel puri is a standout - like many of the dishes here it mixes tangy, spicy, sweet and sour flavours. Best of all they have the oddest pricing you've ever seen. It fair gladdens the heart to see underused figures such as 67p and £1.51 getting their moment in the sun. So three cheers for £2.91 (cumin rice), £6.07 (dhokla) and 87p (mango chutney). Hurrah!

Terre à Terre

71 East Street (01273) 729051
Mon-Fri 12noon-10.30pm, Sat 11am-11pm,
Sun 11am-10pm
Main course around £15
www.terreaterre.co.uk

Terre à Terre offers excitement for the discerning and adventurous vegetable-lover. With a slew of awards and accolades to its credit and dishes that taste like they've been invented in the laboratory of some mad genius, the restaurant has almost single-handedly raised the bar for vegetarian food in the UK.

A beloved Brighton institution with a casual, friendly atmosphere, its clientele covers immense, tattooed bikers chowing down on the famous Beets and Bigarade rosti and yoga instructors serenely savouring the Better Batter and Lemony Yemeni Relish (Terre à Terre's take on traditional fish and chips). Sometimes the punning dish names can get a bit much - How's Ya Vada and A'right Treacle for instance − but there's no denying the food's startlingly complex flavours.

Our recommendation? Start with the Terre à Tapas sharing plate - a great way for the newcomer to sample the wonderful variety of tastes on offer - and then try one of the mouth-watering main courses with an unpronounceable ingredient or two. **Cheeky tip:** walk-ups are welcome during the week (before 8pm is your best bet) but if you're thinking of visiting on Friday or Saturday, book at least two weeks in advance.

MY BRIGHTON & HOVE

Name: DAVE 'The Wedge' WEDGE bus driver

1. Western Road between Montpelier and Waterloo Street I bloody love this stretch because it offers the chance to burn off cyclists at the traffic lights and leave them for dead behind some parked vehicles, followed by a beautiful open 200 yards where you can pick up a bit of speed and overtake another bus or two, before slamming on the anchors and making one or two passengers stumble drunkenly about and drop their shopping if they've been silly enough to get out of their seats before we reach the stop.

2. Union Road, top of The Level A classic pair of 90 degree turns, first a right hander off the Lewes Road, taken at speed so the passengers on one side of the bus have their faces squashed against the windows, then a rapid sprint to the next lights for a sudden left hander and no worries if the lights suddenly change against you, there's a three second lag on this junction so you can jump the red. When this happens I usually make a little cowboy-style whooping sound.

3. East Street Not really an official bus route I know, but it makes a handy short cut when the Old Steine's all clogged up with taxis. Why they let them use the bus lanes I'll never understand. The going gets a bit rough on East Street when you reach the cobbled bit but it's worth it to see all the surprised pedestrians and fortune tellers jumping out of your way. I like to put my head out the window and shout "*didn't see this coming did yer?!*"

MEET ANNA AND CRAIG...

NORTHERNERS DOWN SOUTH

HOW TO MAINTAIN YOUR NORTHERN-NESS IN A SOFT SOUTHERN CLIMATE

GOT NO MONEY?

ARE YOU NORTHERN?

THERE ARE **BARGAINS** TO BE HAD...

WE LIKE BUSY FRIENDLY PUBS.. AFTER A FEW PINTS ANYONE WILL TALK TO YOU DOWN HERE, TAKE ADVANTAGE!

👍 **Foundry** Foundry Street

👍 **Lord Nelson** Trafalgar Street

👍 **Evening Star** Surrey Street

👍 **Basketmakers** Gloucester Road

FOOD FOR A FIVER OR LESS... GET IN!

👍 **Pompoko** *a quick tasty meal in a jiffy* Church Street

👍 **Iydea** *post 4.30pm: discount takeouts of tasty/filling vegetarian food* Kensington Gardens

👍 **Carlito Burrito** *£5 a burrito on a lunchtime* York Place

👍 **Burger Brothers** *Best Burgers in town* North Road

KEEP IT SAFE – WEAR FASHION THAT'S BEEN TRIED AND TESTED...

INDEPENDENT RAG

👍 **Dirty Harry**

👍 **Independent Rag**

👍 **To Be Worn Again**
all three on Sydney St in the North Laine

Or if you're here on a Sunday
👍 **the market on top of the car park by the Marina** *get the no7 bus from town*

FED UP OF FORKING OUT FOR CHEAP SXXXX THAT SWEDES HAVE MADE, GRAB SOME FREE OR DEAD PERSON'S FURNITURE:

👍 **Car boot sale** Sunday on top of the car park by the Marina *Get the no 7 bus from town*

👍 **Markets and flea markets** in the North Laine around and about Upper Gardner Street *especially Saturday*

👍 **Outside people's houses** yes just left there for you to take!

👍 **Snoopers Paradise** Kensington Gardens *an emporium*

CREATE A SMALL CHANGE EMPIRE THE STREETS ARE LITTERED WITH SMALL CHANGE... MONEY TO BURN DOWN HERE!

105

Photographer: Andrea Shamlou   Designer: Matthew Balaam

Restaurants

There are more than 400 restaurants in Brighton, with cuisine ranging from African, Mexican, Asian, Japanese and Lebanese to Greek, French, Italian... even English. But as the food served up in this town varies wildly in quality (not to mention quantity), this chapter offers up the most characterful places, combined with a range of styles and prices to suit everyone's pockets. So, after all this hard work, not to mention putting on 200 pounds in the process, we'll be very annoyed if you end up in McDonald's.

A FEAST FOR THE EYES

Bom-Bane's

24 George Street, Kemptown
(01273) 606400
Tue and Thur 5pm-11pm,
Wed 12.30pm-11pm, Fri 5pm-11.30pm,
Sat 12.30pm-11.30pm
Stoemp and sausage £10
www.bom-banes.co.uk

Nothing short of magical, Bom-Bane's is one of our favourite places in Brighton. Set up by talented performer Jane Bom-Bane, this is a two-storey restaurant offering modestly-priced food, much of it Flemish influenced, with a superb selection of sausages and a range of Belgian beers to match.

Eating on the ground floor, you'll have a chance to marvel at Jane's own creations, unusual tables that invoke the spirits of Wilf Lunn and Willy Wonka: some contain beautiful models of Brighton, some seem to move of their own accord, while others set off eerie chime bars when you... well, we'll leave you to discover that for yourself.

Plus, Jane is a charming performer, prone to wearing eccentric hats, singing harmonium-soaked songs (*"There's a Goldfish Bowl on my Head"*) and reciting poems. She also serves up weekly cabaret, film and food nights. Despite only seating 20-odd people downstairs, Jane somehow manages to coerce performers of the calibre of Stewart Lee, Robin Williamson (Incredible String Band) and Jerry Dammers to perform here.

A particularly good time to visit is during the May festival when every night there'll be shows on and usually something written by Jane and with an all-star cast of performers, often including the staff. What other restaurant could demand "the ability to sing well" as a pre-requisite to working there or boast that your spoons will have been played before you eat your pudding?

Highly recommended.

Chilli Pickle

17 Jubilee Street (01273) 900383
Mon and Wed-Sat 11.30am-4pm,
6.30pm-10.30pm, Sun 11.30am-4.30pm
Mains £12-£17
thechillipickle.com

A far cry from the British curry house of old with its tightly packed tables and prison-break lighting, Chilli Pickle is spacious, woody, softly illuminated and somehow mixes a timeless elegance with the feel of a cared-for canteen. This casual setting however, belies the ferocity of imagination at work in the kitchen, which covers a multitude of Indian cooking disciplines; they started by corralling staff from Kerala, Kathmandu and Nepal, and

Jane Bom-Bane wearing a little something she just threw together

now have over ten regional speciality chefs, while the dishes just seem to get better year after year. Expect the likes of red tandoori sea bream, chilli monkfish, Mysore masala dosa and Indian gourd and paneer dumplings, with many dishes presented on banana leaves. Beverages include a good range of craft beers and wines but we recommend also trying their traditional and exotic soft drinks that include lassis and coolers, flavoured with mango, rose syrups, pomegranate and ginger.

For some, the real star of the show here is the lunchtime street food menu, a kind of exotic Woolworth's (RIP) savoury pic-n-mix where you can fill your face with a stupendous variety of flavours. There's also a street food cart outside for those who want lunch on the hoof.

Moshimo

Bartholomew Square (01273) 719195
Daily 12noon-11pm
Dishes from the belt £1.90-£6
Sushi sets £10-£15
Tasting menu £25.50
moshimo.co.uk

First impressions of Moshimo are stunning: situated in the small square by Brighton's Town Hall, this is a futuristic-looking screened cube with outdoor seating. Inside, between wooden-slatted floor and textured ceiling a great conveyor belt of tempting delicacies snakes around light rattan benches and a long bar. When something tasty-looking passes by, you pick it up. (It may turn out to be pickled octopus with horseradish, but you can always hide it in your pocket if you don't like it.) On the menu are sushi and sashimi sets on stylised chopping boards, tofu dishes, a variety of hot meat dishes and a Moshimo tasting box if you fancy sampling a bit of everything.

Rarely in Brighton has a cuboidal conveyor-belt style Japanese restaurant courted so many contrary opinions – friends either rave or gripe about it, but we've always found the food to be of great quality here and while service can be a little hit and miss, it's nothing to get your knickers in a twist over. This is a restaurant with a good selection of Japanese food and a big personality.

Cheeky tip: become a member and you get huge discounts Monday and Tuesday. Get there early though, these nights can be super-busy at times.

64 Degrees

53 Meeting House Lane (01273) 770115
Daily 12pm-3pm, 6pm-9.45pm
Main (tapas-style) dishes £6-12
(three per person recommended)
64degrees.co.uk

There's no worries about stealing your boyfriend's chips at 64 Degrees – a restaurant that prides itself on a different approach to our traditional British dining habits – as sharing dishes here is actively encouraged. It could almost be English tapas were it not for the fact that each dish is delivered individually to allow time for the flavours to be shared and enjoyed. An ever-changing menu comprises four lots of meat, veg and fish dishes that could include Wasabi lobster croquettes, red mullet and seaweed, ox-tongue pea and pancetta, beef fillet turnip and grapefruit or even chocolate and Horlicks ice-cream. The food here is exquisitely prepared and will delight even the most sophisticated palate.

To experience the best of this restaurant we recommend getting a seat at the pass, the metal counter overlooking the chefs. Here you'll also get to watch the food being prepared and play 'can you guess what it is yet?' as the chefs piece together colours and textures that might look like an omelette with green ice cream but turns out to be crab with beetroot relish. Despite the pressure of being on show the chefs are more than happy to suggest dishes for you, explain their creations or, by special request, perform juggling tricks with two salt cellars and a kitchen knife.

64 Degrees claims to be different to all other British restaurant. A grand claim perhaps, but one we're more than happy to validate at Cheeky Towers. Heartily recommended.

Thewitchez Photo Design Café Bar

16 Marine Parade (01273) 673652
Food served Tue-Fri mid-afternoon till
9.30pm, Sat 12noon-9.30pm,
Sun 12noon-5pm
Mains £9-£17
www.thewitchez-cafe.co.uk

What the ruddy duck is this doing in our restaurant section you may be wondering? Despite the name, this actually is a restaurant that also happens to contain a photographic studio where you can get your passport photos done or take home a mug, tee shirt or pair of knickers bearing a photo of your auntie. The staff (the titular Witchez) are as kooky as their establishment, extremely friendly and proud of their food, which hovers largely around north east Europe with the occasional migration to the Mediterranean. Robust dishes include 'little hooves' (potato dumplings that come in savoury or sweet versions), rosti, beef stew, schnitzel, and Polish or German sausage or you can seek safety in pizza, albeit rectangular and served with "Thewitchez broth." This isn't fine dining but it is very good food creatively presented, and such is the vibe instilled by the candle-lamps and chattiness of the staff, you'll feel as if you've just popped round to a friend's for dinner. Admittedly, a slightly eccentric friend who keeps a giant model witch called Greta propped in the corner of their living room, but still…

Cheeky tip: dog-owners take cheer, you can bring Spot along for dinner if you want, or just say hello to the resident pooch Mr Shadow.

Brighton Pagoda

Brighton Marina, West Jetty, opposite the
Seattle Hotel (01273) 819053
Daily 12noon-2pm and 6pm-10.30pm
Set three-course menu £20-£28 per head
www.brightonpagoda.co.uk

This can claim, without fear of
contradiction, to be Brighton's only
floating restaurant. There is no point in
living if you don't experience the odd
sensation of sampling good Chinese
food as the waves rock you to and fro
(unless you're the kind of landlubber
who only has to look at a boat to
start feeling queasy).

There are no quirks to the menu
but its quality fare given how cheap it
is – you might expect to pay double
for the ambience alone. The waiting
staff can be a tad pushy on a Saturday
evening but be firm and they'll let you
go at your own pace. A wonderful
place to surprise somebody with –
the lower deck is especially romantic
for newfound loves. If you want to
impress without breaking the bank,
this exotic little one-off can be just
the ticket.

La Capannina

15 Madeira Place (01273) 680839
Daily 12noon-2.30pm, 6pm-11.30pm
Main course around £10

You'll be hard-pushed to find a proper
Italian restaurant in these parts
that can match La Capannina's high
standards. It's a genial family-run place
that simply sets store by doing things
the way they did in the old country.
The food is cooked in a wood-fired
brick oven and, unlike some Italian
restaurants, not everything here is
dressed with rocket. The place itself is
atmospheric, romantic (fresh flowers on
every table) and as traditional as they
come. The menu is vast, the choices
familiar and unchallenging (pizza, pasta,
spag bol, gnocchi etc), the food top
quality and the portions gargantuan.
Incredibly good value considering the
standard of cuisine and service, this
genuinely ranks as one of the best –
and let's face it there are some bloody
awful Italian's in Brighton so do yourself
a favour and get your lasagne fix here.

Mange Tout

81 Trafalgar Street. (01273) 607270
Open all day, evening bistro Thurs-Sat
till 10pm
Mains £13-£17
www.mangetoutbrighton.co.uk

Whether you parlez Franglais or not,
the welcome is always chaud here
– none of your traditional stuck-up
Parisian waiter attitude – and if you
express interest in the ever-changing
selection labelled Vin Du Moment then
you will learn all you ever wanted to
know about natural wines and why
Mange Tout (and their lovely sister
restaurant/bar Plateau in the Lanes) are
so obsessed with them. In fact we've
drunk wines here that were so good
we got straight on the internet when
we got home and ordered a case.

While well known for their high
quality breakfasts, where Toulouse
sausage sneaks its way in between
your eggs and bacon, it is as an evening
bistro that Mange Tout really shines.
The food is most definitely south of La
Manche, but more modern than the
heavy cream sauce dishes that came to
define the British experience of such
things in decades past. Amongst the six
or so dishes that make up the menu
on any given day you might find Gallic
classics like confit cassoulet, or less

familiar combinations such as seared cod fillet with almonds and spaghetti made of seaweed, or scallops and roe laced with sumac. Vegetarians are well catered to with at least a couple of imaginative selections, and desserts are familiar but well made, like fruit tarts, coffee panna cotta or cheeses. They like their local ingredients, the meat is Sussex free range, and they know how to cook it. Even better, the portions are generous and you may have difficulty rising from your chair at the end of the meal.

There are a lot of groovy new restaurants in Brighton these days, subscribing to various Heston Blumenthalesque trends or serving your beef cheek in an old football sock. Mange Tout proves that there's no substitute for great simple food served with lashings of bonhomie. One of the best restaurants in town.

"Ok, who wants to kill it?"

Semolina

15 Baker Street (01273) 697259
Wed-Sat 12noon-3pm 6pm-10pm,
Sun (roasts only) 12noon-6pm
Mains £11-£18, lunch set menu two
courses £12, three £15
www.semolinabrighton.co.uk

Previously home to a succession of Indian restaurants, these tiny premises now house a café bistro run by husband and wife team Orson (cooking) and Linda (pretty much everything else). Focussing on local ingredients and making every single item on the premises, they come up with elegantly presented dishes with interesting twists - your pan roasted wild bass comes with summer soup for instance, an exotic Egyptian condiment called dukkah is used to spice up your lamb and even the bread is accompanied by rather decadent truffle butter. On a Sunday they submit to local tradition and serve an absolutely cracking roast lunch - it's actually a better bet than a pub given that they throw in a glass of wine with the set menu. Thanks to a tie-up with expert local wine merchant and bon vivant Henry Butler, the wine list is extremely well chosen, cliché free and priced at pre-Cleggmania levels - it starts at a barely believable £15. In fact the pricing overall is pitched at a level you rarely see in Brighton now for this quality, and even students are occasionally drifting in to spend whatever cash they managed to cadge off their parents before term started.

Semolina is at its best in the evening when it's cosy and inviting, the lighting is dim and in common with many restaurants these days you'll need a torch to read the menu. In the burgeoning London Road scene, this is a medal-winning eaterie.

Carlito Burrito

12 York Place (01273) 671191
Mon-Thur 5pm-11pm, Fri-Sat
12noon-midnight, Sun 12noon-10pm
12 inch burrito or pair of tacos £6-£8
carlito-burrito.co.uk

First the bad news: you cannot reserve a table here unless you are a large party. That, dear reader, is discrimination against couples and people who don't have many friends. The good news is that, if you can cajole the Brighton Bears, Seagulls or Polyphonic Spree to join you, this 'Mexican owned by a Mexican' doles out sensational street food. The rule with the food here is that if you can't pick it up with your hands then they don't sell it, so yes it's the classic offerings of burritos and tacos, and side orders of refried beans and the like. There are however one or two unusual and tempting main items such as mackerel ceviche and a thing with cactus leaves in it. Quite simply the best Mexican food ever served in Brighton.

Kambi's

107 Western Road (01273) 327934
Meze platter £11, mains from £10
www.kambis.co.uk

Discreetly tucked away behind the kebab takeaway shop front, this unassuming, and to be honest fairly uninspiring room actually serves terrific Lebanese meze platters, lamb and chicken shawarmas and assorted charcoal grilled delights. It's a place to go with friends who you trust not to snaffle all the spicy lamb sausages in one go, as you really need to share everything - the mains are absurdly huge so best not to order one each, just get a bit of this and a bit of that. We recommend the kibbeh shamieh, deep fried lamb meatballs, and the unfortunately named foul, which confounds expectations by being a thoroughly tasty combo of mashed broad beans, garlic and cumin. Veggies have a good few choices, though it helps if you really love aubergines. And if you have a spare corner by the end their sugary syrup laden pastry desserts are spectacular.

RESTAURANTS

You can stuff yourself as full as a Lebanese snake charmer's cushion without coming close to worrying your bank manager, not least because they still don't have an alcohol licence even after all these years, so it's BYO and they don't even charge corkage! If you're from Doncaster you'll be here every week, rubbing your hands at the pennies you're putting in your piggy bank.

Pompoko

110 Church Street 07796 001927
Open till 11pm weekends
pompoko.co.uk

The late Brighton presenter/performer Pete McCarthy once wrote: *'never knowingly eat anywhere with laminated menus.'* He may have had a point but there are always exceptions. Pompoko is one of them. Run with supreme efficiency, it serves quality Japanese fast food with most meals under a fiver and a bring your own booze policy. As such, it has to be one of the cheapest and best value eateries in town and is often frequented by local Japanese. It's classic fare: rice, noodle and curry dishes with tofu, meat, fish and occasionally eel, with simple marinades of ginger, soya, sesame oil, and honey.

Food is rarely more than five minutes away, no matter how big the queues. Most times of the day there's somewhere to sit, though you might be jostling for elbow room on the downstairs tables. So, not really the place for a romantic date, particularly given the somewhat stark lighting

— nobody's ever said *"darling your eyes look beautiful by fluorescent tube light"* — but more the perfect stop off when you need to eat quickly and cheaply and prefer the idea of a barley tea and chicken nanban-don to a soggy burger.

Sukhothai Palace

62 Middle Street (01273) 748448
Mon-Sat 11.30am-11pm, Sun 11.30am-10pm
Main course around £8-9
11am-5pm two course lunch menu £4.95
www.spalace.co.uk

"I've had, the Thai of my life, yes, I've never felt this way before…" as the hideous song nearly went. And they so easily could have been singing about this little charmer of a restaurant. The proprietess, a lady called Oy (we think that's how it's spelled), seems committed to the freshness and quality of her ingredients, which at the end of the day is what lifts Sukhothai over the heads of most of the competition (they even pride themselves on being MSG-free). And while a cosy, homely atmosphere pervades, it always seems busy here, even at lunchtimes – which is the best advert a restaurant in this over-provided city can have and due in part to their amazingly good-value two-course set lunch for a staggering £4.95!

The ideal spot for a sneaky midweek date, followed by a couple of pints at the Hop Poles over the road. And where else can you shout to the proprietor, *"Oy! What's for dessert?"* and get away with it?

GO FISH!

Aguadulce

10 Kings Road (01273) 328672
Tue 5:30pm-11pm, Wed-Fri 2:30pm-11pm,
Sat 1pm till late
Tapas from £4, mains £11-£18, paella £15
www.aguadulce-restaurant.com

Don't be put off by the discouraging exterior that makes this restaurant look as if it closed down years ago - this is the most authentic Spanish food you can get in Brighton. There's a fairly impressive range of both tapas and mains available, with an enthusiastic nod to the sea: octopus, clams, crab and even shark get a look in.

With a bar on the left hand side that's often filled with real actual Spanish punters having a terrific time knocking back the sherry, you might feel a bit left out next door in the slightly less invigorating environs of the main restaurant. The solution is to order more of their rather good cava and create your own party with competitions to name-the-straw-donkey (every good Spanish restaurant has one and this place is no exception) and who can do the most appreciative aroma sniffing whenever a new dish is brought to the table. Before you know it you'll be dancing round a sombrero and wondering if you've got sunburn. Happy holidays.

English's of Brighton

29-31 East Street (01273) 327980
Mon-Sun 12noon-10pm
Set menu £17-£22, luxury seafood platter
£35 per person
www.englishs.co.uk

Unchanged since it opened in 1946, and housed in three old fishermen's cottages in the Lanes, English's is both an eat-at-the-counter oyster bar (which still has the original marble counter-top) and a high-calibre seafood restaurant.

There are some nice touches to the service – we love the fact that the waiters present the desserts on a silver tray to help you choose. And the clientele ranges from young couples and seafood fanatics to flirty gay men and groups of old duffers swapping anecdotes about going to school with Denis Compton.

Incidentally, should you end up seated downstairs near the window in the Red Room, have a good look at the mural closest to you. The original owner, Clifford Lee Jones, is the guy pictured holding a glass of wine. Look carefully at the other characters, however, and you'll notice they all look strangely similar. Apparently the artist could only afford one model, hence the eerie Boys from Brazil experience.

Fashions come and go in Brighton but sitting by the window of English's with a bowl of lobster bisque, eavesdropping on three old queens at the table behind and watching the riff raff eating pizza at the restaurant next door, has to rank in the top five quintessential Brighton experiences.

Top tip: despite the many meat dishes on the menu, this is really not their forte and you may end up ordering part of a sheep that appears to have been pre-emptively detonated by the army. Stick to the fishes and invertebrates.

The Little Fish Market

10 Upper Market Street (01273) 722213
Tue-Sat 7pm-10.30pm, and Sat 12noon-2pm
Tasting menu £50 for five courses
thelittlefishmarket.co.uk

With a pedigree that includes The Fat Duck and Marco Pierre White, you would expect chef Duncan Ray to lay on something special, and that is exactly what he does, with exquisitely prepared fish dishes that do something a little different with familiar ingredients. Crispy oyster, parsley flavoured pasta and smoked mushroom are just a few of the delicious creations that provide a counterpoint to the main ingredient. And the quality of the fish is exceptional. But with all the 'food theatre' and ego tripping going on in some Brighton restaurants these days where the chef gets a round of applause for marinating an artichoke, it is refreshing to note that the cook stays out of the way downstairs in the kitchen (until he's finished cooking anyway) while the personable and occasionally cheeky Robert takes care of the diners with an easy professionalism. It's rare to find a place where the phrase high end applies equally to the food and the service.

Relaxed and unstuffy, with a picturesque backstreet location near The Old Market that the shouting hordes of Western Road tend to avoid, this tiny restaurant is a treat for all the senses and undoubtedly the best piscine dining experience in the city.

Cheeky tip: bring plenty of cash; they don't accept cards.

BRIGHTON SMOKED SALMON

The Regency Restaurant

131 Kings Road (01273) 325014
Mon-Sun 8am-10.30pm
Main courses £5-£15
www.theregencyrestaurant.co.uk

Yet another essential Brighton experience – sitting outside the Regency fish restaurant with a good plate of haddock, chips and mushy peas and wishing the i360 would go away. Particularly recommended are their seafood platters: they're excellent value and the calamari can be chewed without having to take out dental insurance.

Curiously, the restaurant next door, the Melrose, has similar prices, menu and style, and as such we've never been able to figure out why the Regency is always much, much busier. Some friends reckon the food is better in the Regency but having eaten at both umpteen times we think there's nothing between them.

If you're after an inexpensive sit-down fish-and-chip dinner with plenty of choice and a sea view, forget Harry Ramsden's and come here instead.

The Salt Room

106 Kings Road (01273) 929488
Lunch 12noon-4pm, dinner 6pm-10pm
(10.30pm Fri and Sat)
Starters £8-£12, most mains £18-£32
www.saltroom-restaurant.co.uk

Replacing a fairly awful bar and diner that used to occupy this appendage to the Metropole Hotel, The Salt Room is the follow up venture to the hugely successful Coal Shed just round the corner in Boyces Street. Both have the same approach, namely a big focus on slabs of meat and fish slapped on a charcoal grill. The difference is that The Salt Room leads with fish rather than steaks, and lobs in a few other ideas like scallop ceviche and fish burgers. There's no denying the high quality of the main ingredient here and they torch it well, though the accompaniments are not always as successful – pickled vegetables need to have more than just a passing acquaintance with vinegar and spices – and at these vertigo-inducing prices every single thing should really be right on the button. You still have to love the imagination and care that goes into their Taste Of The Pier dessert, where miniature doughnuts, candy floss sticks, edible pebbles and the like are scattered across a piece of reclaimed pier walk-board. Ambience-wise it's very modern and rather reserved; the lighting is so low that the pale grey lettering on the menu might as well be written in invisible ink, but if you fancy a better view of where your food came from, there's a front dining terrace, where you can just about see the sea round the back of the i360.

to the London Road end of Brighton. They've been here since 1926, and as well as the chip shop staples there's unbattered specials from skate to sea bass. Eat here once and never again will you be able to face the polystyrene-flavoured fish and cardboard chips they dish out on the seafront. For maximum effect it's best to eat in.

True, there are no French waiters to rush over and top up your mug of tea or sprinkle yet more salt on your chips, but you can stare out of the window here and reminisce about the old hairdresser Mr Cooper who used to work opposite and do haircuts for 100p. Or you could even plan what puppy you're going to buy from the pet shop next door.

GOOD BUY MR CHIPS

Bankers

116a Western Road (01273) 328267
Mon-Sun 11.30am-10pm
www.bankersrestaurant.com

An excellent takeaway and sit-down chippy, Bankers' fish and chips are near-perfect, they offer decent portions for the price and the fish can even be cooked in Matzo meal (a Jewish alternative to batter and definitely worth trying). If you're still feeling peckish afterwards, *you are a glutton*, but we can recommend the cheesecake.

Bardsley's

23 Baker Street (01273) 681256
Tues-Sat 12noon-3pm, 4.30pm-9.30pm
www.bardsleys-fishandchips.co.uk

Arguably the very best in town and well worth the long hike from the sea

PRESTON STREET

Despite the glut of restaurants in Brighton, if it's Saturday night, you're in town, hungry and have forgotten to book somewhere to eat, you could be in trouble. One of your best bets therefore is to head for Preston Street (which runs from Western Road to the seafront): it contains more restaurants per square inch than anywhere else on the face of the earth. They are of varying quality (so please don't blame me if your steak tastes like an old pair of Campers) but you do have an incredible choice of Chinese, steak houses, Italians, Japanese, Indians and countless others. And if you don't like food at all, there's always The Dirty Squid on the seafront.

Watering Holes

Chances are that during your time in Brighton you might be tempted to pop for a swift half somewhere, so you'll be pleased to know that we have enough pubs and bars in the city to satisfy even the thirstiest of Glaswegians: from the tiniest (Queensbury Arms) and the tackiest (anywhere on West Street), to the campest (Regency Tavern).

This chapter contains a carefully chosen selection of pubs and bars that not only cater for all you fresh-faced hipsters but are also welcoming to the merely young at heart. Cheers.

Or "Bottoms up", as they say in Kemptown.

KEY TO PUB LOCATIONS

C	- City centre
Ha	- Hanover
H	- Hove
K	- Kemptown
L	- London Road
NL	- North Laine
OL	- Old Lanes
S	- Seafront
SD	- Seven Dials
X	- Xanadu
Z	- Brighton Zoo

CLASSIC LOCAL BOOZERS

The Basketmakers Arms (NL)

12 Gloucester Road (01273) 689006
Food served 12pm-9pm
basket-makers-brighton.co.uk

Cherished by long-term residents, the Basketmakers is simply a damned good local with no frills, no pumping music, no super-strength lagers, no vile artwork on the wall and plenty of decent pub grub. And, hidden away in the backstreets of North Laine, it's a place that weekend revellers rarely stumble across.

Part of the Basketmakers' unique charm lies in the thousands of old tins that cover the walls from top to toe, in which you can leave messages or look for any that have been left.

We hid one in the Huntley & Palmers Dundee cake tin in 2002 (though we can't guarantee it'll still be there now) and found another with the message "Simon Amphlett cooks smelly kippers all the time. And liver. PIG'S LIVER. I do not approve" in a puncture-repair kit

CALL ME FOR A
POLITE CONVERSATION
07981591761 ⎰ Please
    OR ⎱ Leave
07733317027 ⎰ Here

tin. Other finds over the years include the message *"Ruth Hutt licked my face"* (?). Or how about the photo of this woman (top right) with the message on the back: *"Please help us find this woman"*.

If you visit the pub it is your sworn duty to continue this fine tradition, particularly if taken with the urge to write fruity comments about other customers, such as this discovery: *"The man in the black dress coat needs to ring Kate or have sex with her and then leave"*. Lately we've been coming across some peculiar but rather fetching drawings and even found a seven-inch vinyl single crammed into a container up near the ceiling!

The Barley Mow (K)

92 St Georges Road (01273) 682259
Food served 11am-10pm

While in need of a little TLC and a
spring clean, the Barley Mow has a
big heated beer garden to keep the
smokers happy, a fine range of ales,
free board games and an old-school
tuckshop selling the likes of Flying
Saucers and Fruit Salads. Where else
in Brighton could you have a pint of
Harveys with a banana candy top?
Guinness and Chomp chaser? Malibu
and Kinder? Its real selling point
however is that it does roast dinners
most nights until 10pm (phone ahead
to check) which might not be gastro
pub standard but are hearty fare.
Plus it's the only pub in Brighton –
or perhaps in the world – to have
a 'sperm table'. But you'll have to
discover what that is for yourself.

The Battle Of Trafalgar (C)

34 Guildford Road (01273) 882276
Food served weekdays 12noon-2.30pm,
weekends 12noon-5pm

Once the hangout for Brighton's
theatrical types, the Trafalgar is a
relaxed, spacious local with plenty
of seats, a suntrap beer garden and
lots of lovely old theatre and comedy
posters from days gone by.

The clientele and staff here have
always been a friendly and mellow
bunch; the chance of witnessing a fight
in this place is about as likely as Elton
John's hair growing back of its own
accord. The bar billiards table has long
since gone (the manager insisted it
was broken but a cheeky local chipped
in that it was due to 'cost-cutting'!) but
as good locals go it's one of
Brighton's finest.

The Colonnade (NL)
10 New Road (01273) 328728
thecolonnadebrighton.co.ukl

This bar helps serve the Theatre Royal next door and is bizarre at the best of times; the atmosphere ranges from that of a morgue to a Simon Callow party, with everyone throwing their arms around each other, shouting — "Darling, I thought you were simply wonderful!" The walls are decorated with signed photos of cheesy celebs (Roy Kinnear, Jeffrey Archer etc) which inevitably steer conversation around to trying to work out who they all are, and if anyone can remember the name of the bloke who played Eddie Shoestring.

While not to everyone's taste, the Colonnade will appeal to anyone who doesn't mind sharing their pub with a barmaid singing along to The War of the Worlds album, a load of hammy actors arguing over whose round it is, Su Pollard trying to coerce a shag out of the assistant manager, and an elderly gentleman in a three-piece suit who, completely unnoticed by all, passed away several hours ago.

And if none of that appeals, at least it's one of the few places in the centre of Brighton where you can pretty much guarantee a seat on a Friday night.

The Cricketers (OL)
15 Black Lion Street (01273) 329472
Food served weekdays 12noon-3pm, weekends 12noon-5pm
cricketersbrighton.co.uk

One of Brighton's oldest pubs, the Cricketers was once a whorehouse and is suitably decorated with red Edwardian-style furnishings, old gramophones, ornate table lamps, stags' heads and wallpaper that'd make your granny blush.

For literary fans and historians a trip upstairs is a must (if it's closed off, ask the barstaff nicely and they should let you take a peek). The Greene Room contains letters and articles from Graham Greene (it was his favourite Brighton boozer and earns a mention in Brighton Rock) while the Jack the Ripper Room is like a mini museum with newspaper articles and photos about a certain Robert D'Onston Stephenson, one of many nefarious characters believed to have been the Ripper, who once stayed here. One article about him lists his hobbies as magic, prostitution and murder, though we somehow doubt this was taken from his work CV.

This pub is best avoided at weekends when it's uncomfortably busy. On a quiet winter weekday however, the Cricketers transforms back to an eccentric aunt's front room where you can bag the window seats by the trophy cabinet, or sit at the back by the fire and admire the chamber pots and gaudy furnishings and quietly pen a murder mystery.

The Evening Star (C)

55/56 Surrey Street (01273) 328931
darkstarbrewing.co.uk/the-brewery

The tap house for independent Dark Star brewery, the Evening Star is the place to come if you're passionate about your beer. As well as offering such heavenly brews as the award-winning Hop Head, Old Cocky and American Pale Ale, the bar props up ten hand pumps (seven for the real ales,

two for cider and one for Horlicks).

Those on the pull be warned, this pub does have its fair share of real-ale types (those who were around long before 'craft' beer, smack their lips a lot and have a leather tankard hanging from their belt) and the average women to men ratio is 1:23, but if you're looking for somewhere to sample some genuinely excellent ales and true Brightonian hospitality, this place will not disappoint. The Evening Star is hugely popular at weekends when it adopts a kind of village-pub feel against a conversational background noise so loud you'll end up having to shout to be heard.

Dress code: Hawkwind T-shirt and beer belly for the guys, crew cut for the ladies.

Cheeky fact: back in 1908 the landlady here gave birth to conjoined twins, Daisy and Violet Hilton. They became the highest paid performers in travelling shows in the US, earning up to $5,000 a week, and later became famous through the Hollywood film Freaks. They were even both married for a short time, which does make the mind boggle about how they all dealt with bedroom etiquette.

The Great Eastern (NL)

103 Trafalgar Street (01273) 685681
Food served Mon-Sat 12noon-11pm,
Sun 12noon-10.30pm

Another unspoiled Brighton pub with old wooden tables, shelves of books at the back, newspapers, friendly barstaff and a genuine mix of clientele from students to beardy old men (we even saw a vicar in here one Sunday necking a pint of Guinness).

If you're coming for the night it often pays to arrive early as seating is limited; the tables facing the bar can get a bit cramped if it's busy, while the big tables at the far end of the pub are perfect if you're bringing a crowd. The Eastern also specialises in American whiskeys, so whether you dig rye, bourbon, or corn, they've got you mashed. If you happened to be rooting for the other side during Pearl Harbour they can even pour you a slug of Japanese whiskey in the form of the excellent (and quite pricey) Nikka From The Barrel.

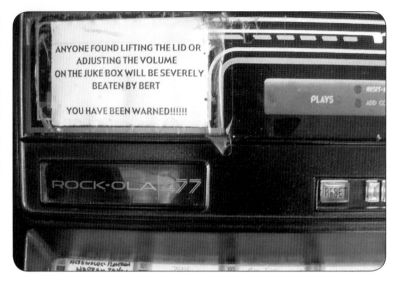

The Hand in Hand (K)
33 Upper St James's Street
(01273) 602521

A one-room, old-school, real ale pub, the Hand in Hand is decorated with newspaper stories (the Kennedy assassination's up there somewhere), has a working one-armed bandit by the door, naked Victorian ladies on the ceiling (pictures, not real ones), a piano that actually gets used, a dusty collection of ties and nearly always a friendly dog or two loping around. All things considered it's one of the town's best boozers. Worth noting is that this is a VERY small pub. Most of the week you'll have no difficulty finding a seat as there'll just be:

a) You

b) A table of students

c) A couple who look like extras from *Last of the Summer Wine*

d) A chap with an eye patch, vintage suit and a passing resemblance to George Orwell. (We also think he's the mystery piano player who dresses as Rowlf from the Muppets in North Laine, but it's just a hunch.)

Top tip: at weekends it can get busy, so prepare to be standing, especially on music nights. It's not so bad though, chances are you'll have a bizarre conversation with a stranger; it's that kind of pub.

The Heart and Hand (NL)
75 North Road (01273) 683320

The marmite of Brighton pubs, you'll either find this antiquated North Laine pub unfriendly, cliquey and cramped or you'll worship the place. If you play in a guitar band it's more likely to be the latter as this remains the hangout for Brighton musos. The reason for this is simple – the pub's famous jukebox, which features the likes of The Seeds, The Misunderstood and Scott Walker.

Weekends in here you can play "spot the bassist from..." as denim-clad blokes with interesting hair spill Guinness down your back while they stand around arguing loudly about the Beach Boys. Juxtaposed with the muso crowd you'll find North Laine traders, old-school antiques dealers, spivs and wrinkly old soaks. Or was that Peter and the Test Tube Babies?

The Lord Nelson (NL)

36 Trafalgar Street (01273) 695872
Food served Mon-Sat 12noon-2.30pm, Sun 12.30pm-3.30pm
thelordnelsoninn.co.uk

Halfway down Trafalgar Street the Nelson is often overlooked, even by long-term residents, which is a pity as – together with the Great Eastern, the Trafalgar and the Basketmakers – this really is one of the best locals in North Laine. With tobacco-stained walls, homemade food, and an unspoken policy of conversation taking priority over music, the Nelson has been spared the makeover treatment and remains a cherished old-school drinking establishment. Hopefully their expansion into the shop next door won't alter things too much.It's also popular with the Brighton & Hove Albion football crowd. Come here of a wet afternoon, sit down with a pint of Harveys Armada, bangers and mash and a copy of The Argus and, within a few hours, you'll be shouting *"Come on you Seagulls!"* in a genuine Brighton accent.

Curiously, for years now a Dungeons & Dragons group has been coming to the Nelson every Monday night dressed up as wizards and goblins and losing themselves in their Tolkienesque fantasy world, though how welcome they are is another matter. An innocent enquiry to the barman – "Do you still have the Dungeons & Dragons here on a Monday?" prompted him to roll his eyes, throw his arms in the air and say, *"look mate, it's got nothing to do with us all right? They just keep bloody turning up".*

Mitre Tavern (L)

13 Baker Street. (01273) 683173
Mon-Sat 10.30am-11pm,
Sun 12noon-10.30pm
mitretavern.co.uk

With the gradual transformation of the London Road area, pubs have either closed down permanently, stubbornly remained too dangerous to drink in, or become civilised yet soulless. Luckily the Mitre continues to buck all hostelry trends that have come and gone since 1982, thanks to Harveys brewery's longest serving tenant Pauline.

Fans of mid-20th century pub styles will be in heaven here spotting the leatherette bench covers, time warp gas fire and pastel nightmare patterned carpet. So determinedly old-fashioned is the pub that it doesn't even accept plastic cards for payment. But the real throwback in this place is the wide range of customers and ages - people over the age of 55 simply don't exist in most Brighton pubs - and the atmosphere of conviviality that seems to engender; nowhere else in town have we experienced other customers bringing us stools to sit on from the other bar.

Top that off with one of the best kept Harveys ranges outside Lewes and you realise that this is an oft-uncelebrated gem that ranks with the Nelson and the Trafalgar for old school drinking style and the days when you could pop to the boozer at lunchtime for three pints, go back to work for an afternoon snooze, and a colleague would wake you up when it was time to go home.

Top tip: don't order the wine.

The Ranelagh Arms (K)

2 High Street, on corner of
St James's Street
(01273) 681634
theranelagh.co.uk

So we walk in here one Easter Sunday to meet friends, and we're confronted by two guys doing the Hokey Cokey to the orchestral break in the Beatles' *A Day in the Life* (?!), while at one of the tables near the bar, a guy is shouting, *"I've taken more acid then every fucker in here. And anyone who says not is a fucking liar!"*

Welcome to another St James's Street anomaly. Sandwiched between gay bars and posh restaurants lies the Ranelagh, the last bastion (in Kemptown at least) of the professional beer belly, blues aficionados and musicians with corrugated faces. Come and meet an array of characters, from friendly middle-aged blokes with ponytails and leather waistcoats to the kind of person one might simply describe as 'alarming'.

The music-themed decor ranges from the quaint to the naff, with albums stuck to the ceiling, pennies glued on the bar, banjos, guitars and accordions everywhere and a few dodgy photos and illustrations of old guitar legends on the walls. The Ranelagh does still pay homage to its theme, offering regular live music, from boogie-woogie pianists to blues guitarists. And this, of course, is the time to experience the pub at its best.

Otherwise, it's the perfect starting point for anyone foolish enough to take the challenge of a Tuesday night 'alternative' Kemptown pub crawl.

The Setting Sun (Ha)

1 Windmill Street (01273) 626192

"This reminds me of being on holiday," said our out-of-town companion last time we visited, and we know what she means. Located at 40,000 feet above sea level near Queen's Park, The Setting Sun is best experienced on a warm summer night when the reason for its name becomes apparent. Its Mediterranean style terrace offers enviable views of Brighton centre and seafront, with Worthing Pier, the Isle of Wight and even Belgium visible on a clear day. What's more there's also now an outdoor snug with trellises, leather sofas and a fire, which regulars have taken to booking ahead, such is its cosiness. Having gone through a slew of managers in recent years, The Setting Sun's new owners, John and Matt, seem determined to make it work, with plans for a firepit for toasting marshmallows, chandeliers and weekend entertainment. Matt, a former BA air steward, says *'I love working in hospitality. A tray's a tray, whether it's in the air or on the ground.'* As such they're keen on offering table service, occasional free shots and even a blanket for anyone getting a bit parky outside on colder nights. After horror stories of the pub's previous grumpy owners, it's clear The Setting Sun has gone through quite a transformation.

FAMOUSLY KNOWN AS

The Hole in the Wall

BRIGHTONS SMALLEST PUB

HIP JOINTS FOR HEPCATS

The Bee's Mouth (H)
10 Western Road, Hove (01273) 770083

Inauspiciously flanked by kebab shops and often camouflaged by a dense throng of smokers, the Bee's Mouth will reward your penetrative persistence once you burrow inside as a moody twilight world awaits.

With cosy booths, trumpet candleholders and spinning heads beneath the bar, the Bee's Mouth feels more like a bohemian hangout from 60s Paris than a Brighton boozer. Squeeze past the bar and you'll find a chilled-out area at the back with a curtained corner for canoodling couples, and if you're feeling brave venture into the basement performance area (Wednesday open-mic nights are pretty wild down here).

The toilet arrangements have been improved over the last few years to include a unisex cubicle in addition to the traditional male and female roles, and it's worth a visit even if you're not bursting, just to view the Steve Buscemi shrine that it contains. We had no idea Steve swung both ways so we've learned something there. The pretty people still make this their drinking den of choice so if you're after an attractive arty crowd, enjoy the occasional slice of far-out jazz, and don't mind rubbing shoulders and probably other body parts too on busy weekends, the Bee's Mouth will deliver.

Highly recommended.

The Black Dove (K)

74 St James's Street (01273) 671119
www.blackdovebrighton.com

A piano suspended in mid-air and a cellar snug that resembles the hold of a ship captained by a kleptomaniac pirate would in themselves warrant closer inspection of the Black Dove. But beneath this eccentric veneer, there beats the broken heart of a proper drinking den. Food is most definitely not served, here it's all about the liquor, the staff and the tunes. William and the team serve up a lesson in amiable bartending along with premium spirits, organic wines and expertly mixed cocktails. And the selection of draught and bottled beers, ales and ciders reads like a Who's Who of celebrity children: from Weird Beard Hit The Lights and Bear Republic Hot Rod Rye to Beavertown

Smog Rocket and Gwatkin Yarlington Mill. They take their booze seriously enough to have a drinks menu on every table — making you wonder why this is not a prerequisite of every self-respecting bar.

Whether delivered by the stereo or outstanding weekend DJs such as Jazzology, the music is a loud and louche mix of jazz, jump blues and Jamaican ska. Regular events include the 'Horseplay' spoken word night and weekly life drawing. Live bands amble in ad hoc and unannounced, though if Tom Waits were ever looking for a Brighton gig we can think of few better-dressed stages than the piratical basement. Then again, perhaps Tom would prefer to take his chances upstairs with a Sazerac rye whiskey and a few choruses of '*The Piano's Been Drinking, (Not Me)*'.

Brighton Beer Dispensary (C)

38 Dean Street (01273) 710624
brightonbier.com

Down a residential side street, a mere pebble throw from Churchill Square, this compact, no frills, real-ale boozer will cater for your hops-swigging habit, away from the city centre riffraff. What they lack in furnishings and finesse, they make up for with great beer from their own Brighton brewery, locally sourced food and enthusiastic facial hair. Formerly the Prince Arthur, the BBP has a main bar room and a cosier conservatory room for serious conversations and board games. For beer, choose from several of their own brews, one of the many bottles behind the bar, or - if you're feeling brave - the 'mystery' light and dark ales next to the one obligatory draught lager (for those who eschew casks of fermented grass, don't worry, they also have cider, wine, whiskey and gin).

The Cyclist (NL)

Brighton Station, Queens Road
(01273) 724879
Mon-Fri 8am-9pm, Sat 9am-11pm,
Sun 9am-10pm
thecyclistbrighton.co.uk

Billing itself as a refreshment room à la Brief Encounter rather than a pub, this newly created railway station bar definitely feels more like a pub, albeit one decorated with expensive junk shop chic. A penny farthing here, an artfully hung blackboard there, some old floorboards repurposed as a wall purporting to be some kind of shed... you get the idea. It's all a refreshing (room) change from the usual soulless corporate outlets that populate our train and plane stations,

THE COCKTAIL SET

Bar Valentino
7A New Road
Classic cocktails with a great upstairs people-watching balcony

Shuffle
27 York Place
Well priced drinks and a smartphone-accessible jukebox for punters to pick from

The Plotting Parlour
6 Steine Street
Posh cocktails in elegant surroundings

Drakes
43 Marine Parade
Hotel bar with menu that tells you what kind of glass your cocktail will fill

Black Dove (see review above)

though you may prefer to drop in for a quick one after a hard day in the Big Smoke rather than spend the entire evening here. They do their best to entice you though, with some decent grub on the menu, pub quizzes (or is that refreshment room quizzes?) and live music nights. And if you've got a bit of a thirst on at breakfast time, they can serve you probably the earliest Campari and soda in Brighton when they open at 8am on weekdays. Something different to dip your croissant in, as Sid James said in *Carry On Up the Pompidou Centre.*

Dead Wax Social (NL)

18a Bond Street (01273) 683844
Open 12-2am/3am
Food served: best to phone, seems to
depend on the sourdough delivery man
drinkinbrighton.co.uk/deadwaxsocial

Shortly before he died, Camus
famously said: *'If Brighton could create
its own god, it'd be a giant turntable
robot thing made of vinyl and it'd talk
like John Peel and organic beer and
pizza would magically appear from two
little hatches underneath its armpits. And*
*it'd have a rockabilly haircut and cool
tattoos. Or something like that.'*

By a curious coincidence, just
twenty five years later the reggae-
themed Riki Tiks in North Laine
transformed into Dead Wax Social, a
cavernous but charming craft beer bar
serving pizzas and honouring the god
of vinyl through the 4,000 records that
fill its shelves. There's a DJ permanently
to hand and he/she'll even give your
latest vinyl purchases a spin (provided

you buy a drink). Vinyl junkies and locals will enjoy spotting photos of familiar faces from the local music scene on the walls, rifling through the records and wrestling with their conscience whether or not to nick the good stuff. Provided the craft beer prices don't have you running to Wetherspoons it's a great place to bring a crowd and either kick off or end the night. Prizes for the first in your group to figure out what the coin-operated device with the lights is, by the bar. If you want a clue, it relates to the fourteenth word in this review.

The Fortune of War (S)

157 Kings Road Arches (01273) 205065
Sun-Thurs 11am-12am, Fri 11am-2am, Sat 11am-3am
www.drinkinbrighton.co.uk/fortune-of-war

This long-established seafront pub gets stupidly busy during the summer weekends when it is mobbed by seafront crowds. In fact, be prepared to experience such a long and

frustrating wait at the bar that you'll wish you'd simply gone to the off licence and headed straight to the beach with some bottles. Come off-season, however, and you'll discover that it's actually a rather cosy bar. Like the inside hull of an old wooden boat, the upstairs has plenty of charm and some good seating areas. If you're in the back of the pub, look up and you'll see the new ceiling boarding where the road above collapsed recently. Don't worry though, they've fixed it now. It's absolutely safe. No, really it's fine.
Top tip: arrive early, bag yourself the window seat with a sea view and you'll be loath to leave.

The Foundry (NL)

13-14 Foundry Street (01273) 697014

Shrugging off its former guise as the distinctly dangerous Pedestrians pub, the tiny low-ceilinged Foundry quickly found its feet with a simple but charming recipe; an open fire, weatherbeaten red leather sofas and chairs, wax and wick powered candelabra, well kept beers, and pizzas and roast dinners. It's always a bit dark and mysterious in here, evoking a warm nostalgic childhood glow from the days when your step-uncle would tie you to a bench outside the pub while he popped in for a couple of pints or five. A refreshingly mixed age crowd fills the place these days, and as one of Brighton's vanishingly rare independent boozers it deserves your support.

The Geese (Ha)
16 Southover Street   (01273) 693491
www.thegeese.co.uk

Now rescued from its 90s incarnation as a semi-Irish and frankly not that exciting boozer that ranked quite some way down the Hanover pub league, The Geese has bounced to the top thanks to landlord Rob, who has brightened up the previously dour decor and brought his winning formula of ultra-chilled atmosphere and sensational bangers and mash menu from The Shakespeare's Head at Seven Dials. It might seem an ordinary

"Chars!"

WHERE TO HAVE A CRAFTY FAG

The ban on smoking has meant getting into pubs can now often mean fighting your way past a gaggle of desperate puffers standing around in the cold unforgiving rain. Smokers of a more leisurely bent may wish to investigate the following places that allow you to sit under cover, usually whilst basking in the fiery glow of an outdoor heater:

North Laine: Prince George (rear), Fountain Head (side), Dorset (front), Colonnade (front)

Old Lanes: Victory (rear), Hop Poles (rear)

London Road: Caroline of Brunswick (rear), Hobgoblin (rear), Park Crescent (rear)

Preston Park: Open House (rear)

Hanover: Dover Castle (rear), Hanover (side), Constant Service (side)

Kemp Town: Barley Mow (rear), Sidewinder (side, of course)

Hove: Lion and Lobster (upstairs)

enough concept but the multiple types of sausage (American Smokey is a favourite, as is the venison), mash, gravy and veg sides are unexpectedly terrific, though our attempts to obtain the recipe for their astonishing proper meat gravy have thus far been rebuffed as "it's a secret, not even the chef can remember how he makes it." There's no garden, but the huge wide windows open onto the street in summer and, if you're as sexually attractive as the Cheeky team, provide ample opportunity for copping snogs off passers by. A triumphant comeback for a pub written off by many.

Northern Lights (OL)

6 Little East Street (01273) 747096
Mon-Thu 5pm-12pm, Fri 3pm-2am,
Sat 12noon-2am, Sun 3pm-12am
www.northernlightsbrighton.co.uk

Set in an old fisherman's cottage, Northern Lights is a dark, welcoming Finnish-run bar-cum-eaterie with

After four pints she's anyone's

a touch of the après-ski. The food is good hearty fare: meatballs in strange brown spicy sauce, open rye sandwiches and reindeer as the star attraction on the menu. But this isn't really just somewhere to eat a nice meal and talk about your new patio; it's a place to hang out, share some tall tales with strangers and sample Icelandic beer or some of the twenty-odd flavours of vodka that range from salty liquorice to Fisherman's Friends. Trust us, they may sound awful but after two shots you'll be hooked. And don't be surprised if, by the end of the night, you're dancing on the tables with your pants on your head.

Cheeky fact: lovers of the supernatural will be delighted to know the upstairs room is haunted by the ghost of a friendly fisherman who can occasionally be heard whispering on the stairs and fiddling with his herring.

Paris House (H)

21 Western Road (01273) 724195
Sun-Thurs 12pm-11pm, Fri-Sat 12pm-2am
the-paris-house.co.uk

While Brighton may have lost its only French church many years ago (the services were actually delivered in French) Francophiles can still play pétanque on The Level, purchase a Breton shirt from Pardon My French in Kemptown and wrap up their Saturday afternoon with a spot of live gypsy jazz at the Paris House.

Its dimly-lit dark wood-panelled interiors, chandeliers, black and white tiled floor and photos of pouting French film stars make for a good setting for a date, post-gig debate (The Old Market is close by) or somewhere to start penning an existentialist novel. Being French themed, there's an interesting wine list, boeuf bourguignon

and rather good platters are on the menu and even the staff speak with a French accent (though whether they're actually French or doing a drama course at A.C.T. is anyone's guess).

One final consideration: with Coopers Cask, Brighton Beer Dispensary and Bee's Mouth a hop and a skip away, it's getting to the point now that a pub crawl down Western Road is not such a crazy idea. Who'd have thought it?

The Watchmaker's Arms (H)

84 Goldstone Villas, Hove (01273) 776307

Welcome to Brighton's very first micropub, a free house concept that's suddenly taken off recently with around 50 opening each year. The idea is to encourage conversation in a largely ale drinking environment, and this conversion of a former electrical retail shop near Hove station does it by banishing any form of piped music or gaming machine. So routine has such noise become, it's a strange but remarkably relaxing experience to walk into a pub and find no background racket aside from the murmur of people talking - and without having to compete with extraneous noise, the customers don't have to talk so loudly, so you only have to hear about Bert's hip operation if you want to earwig deliberately. The Watchmaker's features a simple woody interior, high tables with thoughtfully added coat hooks, and a purpose-built cold room for their constantly changing menu of mainly Sussex ales from independent breweries. If cider is your thing then there's four different ones from Wobblegate to tempt you. And if you prefer wine they have both red and white. And that's your lot so don't come in looking for obscure Siberian vodkas or a schooner of green Chartreuse.

HARVEY'S

Forget fish and chips and sticks of rock, if you want to be a real local, head to the nearest pub and order a pint of Harvey's. Still a traditional family business, Harvey's have been brewing in nearby Lewes for more than 200 years; for those who like a drink or two, a pint of their Best can be synonymous with Sussex, the rolling Downs and lost weekends in Brighton.

Aside from the regular Best there are also many occasional beers. In fact, there's a beer for all seasons: Harvey's Kiss in February, South Down Harvest in September, Bonfire Boy in November (brewed to coincide with Lewes's legendary bonfire celebrations) and Mother-in-Law for winter. The darker (and stronger!) Christmas Ale was recently listed among the world's top 50 beers.

To sample the more interesting brews you need to frequent tied houses such The Lord Nelson, near Brighton station, or the Mitre Tavern, home to octogenarian landlady Pauline Bickell, Brighton's longest serving publican, who still remembers back in the 30s when you could buy a house in Brighton for as little as £250,000. Let's drink to that.

BRIGHTON GIN

After the 2015 election, when Brighton became a green and red dot surrounded by blue, it decided the most sensible thing to do was to declare itself an independent state. Quickly attracting 8,000 supporters and creating its own flag and passport, the People's Republic of Brighton and Hove announced it would be making aid parcels for residents trapped in enemy territory (Tory constituencies), consisting of coffee, yoga mat, seagull relaxation tape and a bottle of Brighton Gin. Thankfully you don't have to be stranded in Hassocks to sample this unique spirit, made in the town's first ever distillery. Brighton Gin, whose botanicals include angelica, lime and milk thistle, can be drunk in dozens of the city's best boozers, from the Bees Mouth and Basketmakers to newbies the Cyclist and Dead Wax Social.

DISCOTHEQUES

Recent years have seen the closure of some of Brighton's more idiosyncratic clubs, like New Hero and Babylon Lounge (though no-one misses the latter). Of course the city is still the go-to for hen and stag nights, and has a thriving student population, both of which sustain clubs with obnoxious names like Shooshh, and tacky beach-themed bars like Lola Lo's and Wah Kiki. However, Brighton's club/DJ scene still boasts everything from cool underground jazz and retro to dubstep and electro nights, as well as hosting the biggest gay club on the south coast. Combine this with regular visits from big-name DJs and it's not surprising that clubs are packed every night of the week.

One of the very special things about Brighton's nightlife is that, unlike so many other UK cities, the clubs here do not merely represent weekend escapism from drudgery and boredom. If anything, some of the best nights here are mid-week, and most venues are refurbished so often that by the time you turn up again on a Saturday the seats will be a completely different colour and the toilets moved to the DJ booth. Clubbing in Brighton seems nothing less than a shameless celebration of living in a party town, which is probably why upbeat and carnival-type music like Latin jazz and Afro-bhangra are particularly popular here. And with club nights celebrating genres from synth-pop to power ballads, the scene has a sense of fun that even Manchester in its heyday could never have provided.

The Arch

187-193 King's Road Arches (01273) 208133
www.thearch.club

Formerly Coliseum, formerly Digital, formerly The Zap, formerly Union, and formerly The Zap again, you have to wonder if their hearts are in it by this point. Besides being a terrible name for a club located between a dozen other clubs in arches, The Arch is aiming to 'revitalise' Brighton's underground house scene. The venue's hefty Funktion-One speaker system has been fully refurbished, and takes up a good third of the main room (although, as in all Brighton clubs, this isn't saying much. Few venues are larger than your nan's front room).

Home to the standard array of student-dominated club nights, The Arch also hosts big-name house DJs and provides a regular slot for up and coming talent. If the music loses your attention, you can always stare at the hypnotic circulation of adverts playing on screens above the bar, showing idealised versions of the night you're trying to enjoy.

Casablanca

3 Middle Street (01273) 321817
www.casablancajazzclub.com

This club specialises in Latin jazz and jazz funk, and is refreshing in that it has live bands and not just DJs. With such a strong DJ culture here, you forget sometimes what a pleasure it is to experience danceable live music, especially when the bands really know how to let rip. True, you might turn up, look at the outside, and think, "oh God, no", and yes, it is cheap and cheerful, but you will have a good time despite yourself.

A CHEEKY TALE

If you look above Patterns you'll see a flat which has a commanding view of the beach and, in particular, the phone box in front of the club. Two guys, Mark and Bruce, used to live up there and some nights after the club had almost cleared out, they'd ring up the phone box, wait for some inebriated clubber to answer, take a note of how he was dressed and then play these weird 50s adverts down the line. It would start with some cheesy music and then go –
"Hi, and welcome to the world of Lux soap, a new powder that'll get your clothes whiter than white"
– and then a different voice would say –
"You are wearing a red shirt, jeans and a blue hat."
Click

If the funky music and those horns *don't* move you to boogie, you're in the wrong city.

Dress code: flares, corduroy cap, goatee.

Coalition
171-181 Kings Road Arches
(01273) 722385
www.coalitionbrighton.com

In its pomp as The Beach this place hosted Fatboy's Big Beat Boutique and Digweed's Bedrock, but you won't find any big names here these days, Other than that, the architectural wonders of the brick arches and pillars tend to be more interesting than the mish mash of trance, funky house, indie, live bands, comedy and hula hooping policewomen.

Concorde 2
Miles from anywhere, Madeira Drive
(01273) 673311
www.concorde2.co.uk

Built out of the ashes of the Water Rats (a one-time greasy bikers' hang-out), the Concorde 2 took over where the original Concorde left off by specialising in live music, cracking club nights (from reggae and punk, house to hip-hop and dirty acid techno) and odd one-offs such as the UK Air Guitar Championships. While the Concorde works far better for live music than club nights it's always fantastically relaxed, reasonably roomy, and you rarely have trouble getting a drink at the bar.

Funfair Club
12-15 King's Road (01273) 757447
www.funfairclub.com

If immersing yourself in a very small ball-pit, already wallowed in by countless other drunks, is your idea of a good time then you're in luck! Aiming to recreate the 'spectacular opulence' of Brighton Pier, Funfair certainly captures that delicate blend of tacky, cheesy and hedonistically enjoyable.

Notable more for its thematic decorations, including carnival cut-outs and the aforementioned sweaty ball pit, than its standard blend of cheerful pop, the place is still worth a look in. Every 'Sideshow' Saturday features circus performers, magicians and entertainers - you'll hear exactly the same music you hear everywhere else, but there might be a lady with a snake.

Funkyfish Club
19-23 Marine Parade, underneath
the Madeira Hotel   (01273) 698331
www.funkyfishclub.co.uk

Like a cow standing alone in a field of sheep, the Fish barely seems to be a club at all in Brighton terms. Insisting on a strict diet of 60s and 70s soul and 'classic' rock, it has no truck with name DJs and attracts a wide-ranging crowd who come to have fun rather than pose. Strict rules have now been imposed on hen parties though, banning matching outfits, bunny ears and "*inflatables of any nature*".

Admittedly, it does have the strong flavour of a wedding reception with its state-of-the-ark lighting, white tablecloths and occasional pensioner, but there's a friendly vibe about the place, even if they will still insist on testing the theory that you can dance to *Sweet Home Alabama*.

Ladies, expect to be chatted up by visiting insurance salesmen staying in the hotel above, who will attempt to make conversation with opening gambits like, "*Oh, yes, I've always been a big fan of Diana Ross and the Pips*".

The Green Door Store

Trafalgar Arches, Brighton Station
07944 693214
www.thegreendoorstore.co.uk

Situated beneath Brighton station, The Green Door Store is far too hip to bother with a sign. The doors are green, which is a helpful clue, but it still feels like you're sneaking into some sort of maintenance area. This impression continues once inside, with the uneven brickwork floor and steel girders left exposed. The bar décor is a schizophrenic mix of country pub - think farm equipment, posters of sheep breeds, tools - and a large neon McDonalds sign. This being Brighton, we're sure the latter is meant to serve as an ironic juxtaposition.

Decor aside, The Green Door Store is an excellent gig venue, with an authentic musty aroma (bricks aren't easy to clean). They put on a variety of events, either free or reasonably priced, and host loads of arty bands, touring and local, that won't disappoint if you're a fan of Pitchfork-endorsed left field music. GDS can also be relied upon for decent club nights, playing a mix of hip hop, RnB, soul, funk, acid house, Reggae, DnB and 50s/60s Rock n Roll. Most underground clubs start and end here. A true Brighton hang out.

The Haunt
10 Pool Valley (01273) 736618
www.thehauntbrighton.co.uk

Occupying the screening room of an old cinema, The Haunt is a decent live venue, where Haim, Rizzle Kicks, Foster the People, tUnE-yArDs and Wild Beasts have all played. It can get very packed, so try to arrive early enough to get a spot on the balcony, or you'll be stuck round the corner from the stage with no view. Otherwise, it's a staple of the student clubbing week, adding more of an indie twist to the regular fare, with nights like Fat Poppadaddys (expect to hear 'Come on Eileen' a minimum of three times). Definitely one for the 'yoof', with tales of 30-somethings being turned away from 'It's Still 1985' for being "too old" (go figure).
Typical fragrance: Lynx body spray and Clearasil.

Patterns
10 Marine Parade (01273) 894777
www.patternsbrighton.com

In 2015 Brighton club Audio was taken over by the ominous-sounding 'Mothership Group', the team behind

The Green Door Store, a place of worship for Shakin' Stevens fans

swish London venues The Book Club, and Stories. Of course Mothership sustained their record of horribly twee names with their latest conquest. The unfortunately named Patterns has been fully revamped to look suitably cool, with lots of light wood, grey concrete floors, and red lighting. The basement club has a new, massive sound system, blaring out a mix of house, techno and what they call 'forward-thinking' electronic music. They get some big names in, like Anthony Parasole, Dave Clarke and Gilles Peterson, but also have a focus on local talent, holding an informal audition process to become a resident DJ. Almost every night of the week has some kind of event on, with Thursdays reserved for Bastard Pop's mix of hip hop and RnB.

During the evenings the bar is a comfortable, if pricey, hang out selling

cocktails and craft beers, with burgers barbecued on the terrace. Patterns also plays host to events like Zine Club and Woody's Colour In Monday Club. These might sound terribly naff, and to be frank they are a bit, but it's actually quite fun doing a bit of arts'n'crafts when you're too drunk to safely use scissors. Altogether, Patterns is proving itself to be much more than just a club.

Pryzm
West Street (01273) 710976
www.pryzm.co.uk/brighton

After spending another million quid on a place that already had millions spent on it just a few short years earlier, Brighton clubbing giant 'Oceana' has completely transformed itself into the totally-indistinguishable-from-how-it-looked-before Pryzm. Aptly described as *"like going clubbing in Disneyland"* by our friend Rick, albeit a theme park where Big Brother seems to be watching your every move to ensure that you only 'enjoy' yourself in the prescribed manner. There are security staff round every corner of this massive venue, herding crowds through the labyrinthine (and hideously patterned) corridors and rooms. Pryzm still hosts a whopping four bars, though sadly Oceana's (relatively) interesting themes have been replaced by such commercial entities as Cîroc vodka. It boasts three dance floors, with a main 'Vegas' room for EDM and House music, the 'Curve' bar playing RnB, and the New York 70s-style disco with the usual array of retro/tacky tunes.

It's easy to get lost and you regularly will, so follow Disneyland child safety guidelines and agree on a Meeting Point with members of your party. Or perhaps you've been to one of the fifteen other identical Pryzms across the country, in which case you'll know what to expect and have brought a map.

Typical fragrance: turquoise Slush Puppy

The Volks

3 The Colonnade, Madeira Drive
(01273) 682828
www.volksclub.co.uk

Hidden away off the main clubbing drag, the Volks is a bit of a gem for its unsniffy attitude and discerning choice of sounds. We've been to some dynamite breaks nights here and there's a host of other specialist fixtures from jungle and afro to DnB, grime and psy-trance. The main room upstairs is surprisingly airy (unlike the downstairs which is about the size of a sheet of A4), packed with excessively friendly people (we left a friend on his own in here and when we came back he hissed *"people keep smiling at me"*) and run by tasteful DJs who, for a change, know how to build a room up rather than throwing the entire bucket of bricks at it from minute one. If there's one carp de diem, it's that there's hardly anywhere to sit down, but then we are getting on a bit. For a taste of the original Brighton underground clubbing experience, this is the one.

Emblematic fragrance: sweat/patchouli.

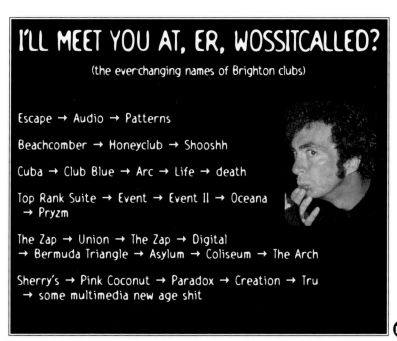

I'LL MEET YOU AT, ER, WOSSITCALLED?

(the ever-changing names of Brighton clubs)

Escape → Audio → Patterns

Beachcomber → Honeyclub → Shooshh

Cuba → Club Blue → Arc → Life → death

Top Rank Suite → Event → Event II → Oceana → Pryzm

The Zap → Union → The Zap → Digital → Bermuda Triangle → Asylum → Coliseum → The Arch

Sherry's → Pink Coconut → Paradox → Creation → Tru → some multimedia new age shit

Entertainment

CINEMAS

See a Hollywood blockbuster on Friday night, the latest David Lynch on the Saturday, then a documentary about voodoo S&M on the Sunday. Here's how.

INDIE CINEMAS

Duke Of York's Picturehouse
Preston Circus 0871 902 5728
Cheaper tickets Mondays
www.picturehouses.com

Found at the end of London Road, this building is pale yellow and has a large pair of stripy legs sticking out over the balcony. It's easy to miss, however, as all the houses on the street have copied the idea and now there are hands, elbows and feet sticking out all over the place as far as the eye can see.

Having celebrated its 100th birthday in September 2010, the Duke's can legitimately claim to be the oldest independent cinema outside London, and shows a fairly wide selection of cult, art house and world films. It has an intimate bar and balcony upstairs and, rather than the usual cinema junk food, offers a fine selection of cakes and hot and cold drinks. The auditorium itself looks magical, with coloured lights around the screen, and the refreshed seating now even has headrests.

The Duke's continues to host some magnificent music events ranging from cutting-edge bands to its annual live *Eurovision* when 300-odd gay men prove they can outdo a whole crèche of ankle biters when it comes to screaming the loudest.

Whether you're a movie enthusiast, music lover, interior designer, cake obsessive or leg fetishist, the Duke's remains one of *the* best reasons for living in Brighton.

Top tips: if you visit the cinema more than four times a year, buy a membership, you'll save loads of money.

A BRIEF HISTORY OF THE DUKE OF YORK'S

The Duke's was originally built for theatrical impresarios Violet Melnotte and Frank Wyatt. Violet, always known to staff as 'Madame', was the archetypal iron fist in a velvet glove and, when one of the actors at the theatre gassed himself, she apparently instructed her solicitor to reclaim the cost of the gas from his estate.

The Duke's famous legs once belonged to a cinema in Oxford known as 'Not the Moulin Rouge' and, every Sunday at 3pm, they do the Can Can.

Duke's at Komedia
Gardner Street 0871 902 5728
Cheaper tickets Tuesdays
www.picturehouses.com

Komedia retreated from their upstairs venue in 2012 to make way for this brand spanking new two screen cinema that brings the Duke of York's "experience" (note to self: this kind of language does not belong in a Cheeky Guide) to North Laine. The grazing element has been amplified with two bars, one downstairs and one upstairs, a bigger range of drinks and hot food like paninis and hotdogs that you carry into the screening on a tin plate. The screening rooms are small (a hundred-ish seats each) with a scattering of sofas for the terminally splayed or the over-affectionate, and you can now book a specific seat when buying tickets. The creation of this cinema has enabled a much wider range of film presentations that often run for just a few days, so there's now even less danger of having to slum it down at the Odeon and even more chance of

catching that Serbian documentary about the history of elastic bands that you were gagging to see on the big screen. While not as gig-friendly as the parent cinema, there are still occasional performances - our friend Jason breathlessly informed us of a recent appearance by Elaine Page, where to his delight she belted out a few of her better known tunes before hurling her underwear at the adoring crowd. Better still, the building has been given its own pair of stripy legs to match those on the original Duke's, except that these ones do the Hokey-Cokey every third Thursday at 8 in the morning. A tremendous addition to Brighton's cultural life.

WHERE TO SEE THE LATEST BLOCKBUSTER

Cineworld

The Marina 0871 200 2000
www.cineworld.co.uk/brighton

Loads of screens and all the latest movies from Tinseltown. You won't find anything adventurous in their billings, and it *is* located below the multi-storey car park in the far-from-glamorous Marina, but serves a need if the Odeon is sold out or you fancy a drive into the middle of nowhere. At weekends you may find yourself ankle-deep in popcorn, teabags and litter. The fact that it seems to be run by young men who still live with their mums has nothing to do with it.

The Odeon

West Street 0333 006 0777
www.odeon.co.uk

The biggest cinema in the town centre and, with Pryzm next door, handy if you're seized by the urge to snog a few teenagers after the film.

ENTERTAINMENT/ THEATRE VENUES

Otherplace at The Basement

24 Kensington Street (01273) 987516
www.otherplacebrighton.co.uk

Deep in the vaults of the former Argus building lies this vast underground space, home to a full range of fringe events, from cult comedy and acoustic music to alternative theatre and spoken-word nights. Programmed by Otherplace Productions, a theatre

company based on the principles of the A-Team (*"if you have a problem, and no-one else can help, and if you can get hold of them…"*), who have hosted some of the comedy world's top talents, such as Daniel Kitson, Josie Long, Robin Ince, Richard Herring, Phil Kay and Pappy's Fun Club, this is *the* best place to catch up-and-coming acts in Sussex. Furthermore, if you've ever wanted to see some new and original theatre, where a small budget is used to sharpen the imagination rather than soften it, then this is the place to go. You also get a chance to mingle with the acts and staff in the bar afterwards, although half of them will probably be out on the pavement having a fag.

Top tip: Otherplace now organise one of the main venues in the

A packed BOAT house

Brighton Festival Fringe, The Warren, They also put on previews for some of the main Edinburgh shows in June and July. They're always on the lookout for new staff and volunteers too, and have good links with other arts organisations, so if you want to get involved in Brighton's arts scene, this is a good place to start.

Brighton Open Air Theatre (BOAT)

Dyke Road Park
www.brightonopenairtheatre.co.uk

The realisation of the dream of local impresario Adrian Bunting, who left his life savings to the project on his untimely death in 2013, BOAT now occupies the site of the old bowling green in Dyke Park. It's a lovely idea to have a dedicated open air space for drama and music, and while perhaps not as extravagant or dramatically situated as Cornwall's clifftop Minack Theatre, it has a green Home Counties charm of its own, plus it's a darn sight easier to get to. Tucked behind bushes

and trees and beautifully realised in timber and AstroTurf (we realise that sounds sarcastic but it isn't meant to be, honest) the tiered amphitheatre seating is surprisingly well insulated from surrounding road noise - you're more likely to be distracted from the show by the warbling of a blackbird than a passing bus. Obviously, the theatre largely operates in summer, but we think there's scope for someone to put on an adaptation of *Singin' In The Rain* at any time of year.

Emporium

88 London Road
www.emporiumbrighton.com

Continuing the grand tradition of converting abandoned sites of religious worship into entertainment palaces, this ex-Methodist chapel now serves as a theatre whose principal purpose is to provide professional productions, ultimately by creating a regional repertory company. They've already got Alan Rickman on board as patron, and in their thus far brief existence have roamed through musicals, panto, a few rather excellent Pinters, and a nicely gruesome portmanteau horror show for Halloween. Monthly media chat show The Space (see later in this chapter) also now calls Emporium home.

The café bar at the front of the building that's supposed to help finance activities is probably the most laid back place to drink in the area (this is still London Road remember, despite the creeping gentrification) and is proving popular with groups of wine-guzzling women and men who wear their overcoats indoors. In an odd reversal of the usual theatrical experience, the auditorium and performance space is actually smaller than the bar, but it's a flexible environment that allows the audience to be placed wherever the show seems to demand. Deserving of your support, even if it's just to buy a proscenium arch-shaped flapjack in the café.

Komedia

44-47 Gardner Street (01273) 647101
www.komedia.co.uk/brighton

Impossible to miss, owing to the fact that its outrageous red lighting turns Gardner Street into an enormous brothel every evening. That aside, god bless the Komedia; we've had many unforgettable evenings here whether it's been getting a nosebleed from listening to atonal jazz group Polar Bear, trying to dance like Siouxsie Sioux at Spellbound or laughing ourselves stupid at Count Arthur Strong's live radio show.

The building of the new cinema upstairs has left Komedia with just their main basement room and the smaller studio out the back, but this doesn't seem to have changed the nature of the events. If anything its improved them - gone are the gruesome tribute bands like Whole Lotta Led Zeppelin ("you're getting great reviews, I wish you the best" - Jimmy Page, royalties

George Egg serves up some hotel room cuisine

beneficiary), and while weekends can get a bit "Jongleurs", there's plenty of other club nights, music, comedy and cabaret to redress the balance. Nights to be championed include Eight Miles High, Pop Kraft, Spellbound, Too Darn Soulful, Synthology and Hammer & Tongue. If you've never been to any of these events, or the Komedia for that matter, it's just possible you might be living in the wrong town.

Latest Music Bar

14-17 Manchester Street (01273) 687171
www.thelatest.co.uk/musicbar

To some, this venue will always be known as the Joogleberry. But while "Latest Music Bar" does sound a bit corporate, at least jokes about dangleberries, fartleberries and the like can finally be buried. Having changed hands a few years ago things did look a little shaky at first but after a cabinet reshuffle in the programming department, all seems to be working out fine. What they've lost in the way of comedy and cabaret, they've gained with live music, as most evenings you'll find local bands, jazz outfits, acoustic sessions or indie bands squeaking around in tight trousers. Other than that, the only real change is that the ground floor now serves as a local TV studio by day, but there's still a magical candle-lit Eastern European-style basement club by night. Just grab a drink, park yourself at a table and marvel at the nighttime scenes of houses with real lights twinkling in the windows that line the walls. And finally, congratulations are due for the best venue website in Brighton. It's simple and informative with good, clear images. What more could you ask of a venue (except for the downstairs loos to be working)?

Brian Gittins and Angelos Epethemeiou, close friends of the rich and famous

JILL EDWARDS

COMEDY WORKSHOPS

www.jill-edwards.co.uk

Ever fancied having a go at stand-up comedy? Jill Edwards comedy course at Brighton's Komedia has a proven continuous track record of success & top TV comedian graduates.

"People say comedy can't be taught. They could learn a lot from Jill Edwards." Jill Edwards Comedy Workshops Graduate - Jimmy Carr

For more information visit www.jill-edwards.co.uk or contact @thejilledwards

Top tip: for those who like spoken word as a change from singer-songwriters, legendary spoken-word nights the Catalyst Club, Café Scientifique and Speaky Spokey can be found here (see later in the chapter).

Rialto Theatre
11 Dyke Road (01273) 725230
www.rialtotheatre.co.uk

One of three new theatres to sprout in the city in the space of just a couple of years, the Rialto provides a permanent home for long-established topical satire night The Treason Show, along with other comedy, theatrical and musical events. Think of it as a kind of mini upside down Komedia without the weekend stags and hens; upstairs is the main space for about 100 people, and downstairs is the Art Deco styled studio bar with less formal seating. You

might find almost anything on here, bar full on music clubnights; flamenco bands, one man shows about Quentin Crisp, or erotic kinky cabaret.

Theatre Royal
New Road 08448 717650
www.atgtickets.com/venues/theatre-royal-brighton/

For the more conservative theatregoer. The Theatre Royal may offer a predictable array of farces, thrillers and musicals starring Tom Conti, Jason Donovan and Su Pollard but for an authentic old-style theatre experience it can't be beaten. The auditorium, with its plush red-velvet seats, is stunning – and they have private boxes for those who really want to do it in style. We once saw Barbara Windsor in the nude here, but that's another story.
Dress code: loafers, slacks and cardie. Monocle optional.

COMEDY & CABARET

The Krater Comedy Club

Weekly at the Komedia (01273) 647101

Running weekends at the Komedia, the Krater follows the tried-and-tested Jongleurs format of compère and three acts. Regularly hosted by local comedian Stephen Grant, known for his speedy delivery, the Krater is unquestionably popular but does demonstrate the frightening lack of original material from most of the comedians currently crawling the national circuit. Attracting stag and hen parties in their droves (an established Brighton epidemic), this is hardly a discerning audience but at least they don't seem to mind listening to desperate single men and women in their mid-30s drone on about masturbation. To be honest, with moronic heckling and mobile phones going off every ten minutes, this is our idea of hell.

Rabbit in the Headlights

Once a month at the Basement, Kensington Street
www.otherplacbrighton.co.uk

A stand-up comedy night for new acts and new material that runs the gamut from glorious success to ignoble embarrassment. Since the night was started in 2005 by Katy Schutte and Tony Harris there have been successes such as Sean Walsh, Brian Gittins and Paul McCaffrey and, erm, quite a few failures. Each act is nominally granted a five to ten minute stand-up slot, though the stage lighting does have to be flashed at any determined ego-mongers who try to remain glued to the stage boards – one truly dire act once managed to stay on for 25 minutes, prefacing every trite remark with 'seriously'. There has also been some most unseemly blubbing on occasion. See some great comedy, witness some life-affirming deaths and most of all, be happy that you aren't up there.

The Catalyst Club

Latest Music Bar
Second Thurs of every month, 8pm-late
www.catalystclub.co.uk

Set up and hosted by the notorious Dr Bramwell, the Catalyst Club is a night for those who enjoy a bit of debate and learning with their glass of wine or beer, as each month the Catalyst plays host to three different guests who speak for fifteen minutes on something they're passionate about.

Talks range from anecdotal stand-up, such as the gentleman whose brilliant and funny talk on *The Persuaders* was really about his 70s childhood, to the challenging ("*Why we should all go to church*" and "*Debunking Quantum Physics*" raised an eyebrow or two) and the fascinating and bizarre – zombies, giant squid, occultism, Tin Tin, naturism and tinned meat have all got a look in.

There's usually a Q&A session at the end of each talk where the audience, and sometimes the bar staff too, chip in with their comments. And if that's not enough, there's often a short film or something. In case you might think we're a little biased, we'll leave you in the capable hands of satisfied punter Tom Sheriff:

"*The Catalyst Club? It's the only night out in Brighton, or perhaps anywhere in the UK, where you can get thoroughly pissed, get free stuff and go home knowing more than you ever thought you could or would need to about such unlikely topics as the history of the martini, the life of Herman Goering and why toast always falls butter side down.*"

Café Scientifique

www.meetup.com/Brighton-Cafe-Scientifique

Long-established science debating club which meets monthly at the Latest Music Bar (or did at time of going to print) and features a talk from a guest scientist, usually clutching his/her latest tome, followed by a one-hour Q&A and a whip-round to pay for some new corduroy. The whole event is very relaxed and informal and can – at times – spark some fascinating debate. Check website for details.

"Join me brothers, let us storm the i360 gift shop."

The Space

Once a month, Emporium
www.thespace.uk.com

A shining example of what you can accomplish through sheer hard graft, The Space is a monthly media and arts event which invites famous creative types to come and talk about their work and ideas. The creation of Wayne Imms (whose phone bill must be astronomical), The Space's list of interviewees so far is incredibly impressive, from Factory Records artist Peter Saville to Barry Cryer, Mark Gatiss and William Orbit. Not only that, it's a good place to socialise and brush up against the guests and the raffle prizes are often sensational.

GAMBLING

Genting Casino

6-8 Preston Street (01273) 725101
2pm-5am daily
www.gentingcasinos.co.uk/casino/brighton

Taking itself more seriously than the Grosvenor round the corner, as you step in and hear the lilting tones of Phil Collins and Philip Bailey singing Easy Lover you'll realise that this place means business. The decor has recently been upgraded from 1983 to 1989 with padded walls, migraine-inducing geometric patterned carpet and a clientele to match – for whom the mullet is still not a fish. But be warned, they have a shoot first ask questions later policy for anyone who cheats.

The Greyhound Stadium

Nevill Road, Hove (01273) 204601
box office 0845 7023 952
Open Wed-Sun, afternoon racing free admission, evening racing £5-6
www.brightonandhovegreyhoundstadium.co.uk

An excuse to don your best tweed cap, dust off Parklife and shout yourself hoarse. Sorry, dog. The minimum bet is only a pound; forget trying to figure out how the betting works, just pick the dog with the silliest name, use the touts outside for better odds, watch out for the lasagne and you'll have a terrific night out. Recommended if you fancy a birthday night out with a difference.

The Grosvenor Casino

9 Grand Junction Road (01273) 326514
24 hours a day, every day. Really.
www.grosvenor-casinos.co.uk

Having long ago moved from its old home by Brighton Station to a swankier residence, this casino has gone decidedly upmarket since the days of grotty psychedelic carpets and a tiny bar. There are now automated roulette tables, a £4,000-jackpot fruit machine, higher minimum stakes, live entertainment some weekends and a bar which stays open longer. True, it's still full of guys with overpowering aftershave trying to impress their white-stilettoed ladies, and swarms of Chinese businessmen with money to burn, but with its massively popular Texas Hold'em poker room, the Grosvenor seems to attract a student crowd as well.

Membership and entrance is still free and as long as you turn up with decent proof of identity you're straight in. And did we really once hear the desk girl say "Good evening, Mr Paradise," to one of the regulars as we were leaving?

MY BRIGHTON & HOVE

Name: NICK PYNN
Brighton's celebrated fiddler, musician, inventor of the Cocolele and all-round good egg

Brighton, Grandad & Max Miller: a short memoir

Grahame Greene's Pinkie Brown grew up in pre-war Nelson Place, as did my dad in real life, the eldest of five and the son of a Brighton bookie. His mum was a court dressmaker and ex-music hall artiste, and his sisters Joan and Lily were dancers. My uncles Harry and Ted were, respectively, a plumber and a dockhand. I remember staying with my grandparents at 279 Albion Street after family weddings. Grandad would always recommend that I smoke a pipe when

Auntie Lily's wedding.
L-R: Max Miller, Frank Pynn

I grew up. He was a bit of a gangster, whom my uncles remembered seeing take out a pistol from a desk drawer when about to attend a 'difficult' meeting. He did however open the first legal betting shop in the south of England.

Music hall performers would attend my grandad's office in Middle Street to bet on a race, before performing at the Hippodrome. Flanagan & Allen, The Crazy Gang, 'Monsewer' Eddie Grey and Max Miller (a close family friend) were all regular customers.

A few years back I was asked to perform with Arthur Brown at the Theatre Royal in a show to raise money for Brighton's Max Miller statue. I asked George Melly, smoking at the stage door, if he'd known Mr Miller, to which he replied, "I bought him 15 brandies once… he didn't buy me one back". My uncle Ted told me that Max gave him a guitar in the 1950s saying, "'ere… my game's finished. Take this and learn it – it'll be the kids with guitars next that'll make all the money…".

The Music Scene

(Upstairs at) The Prince Albert

Trafalgar Street (01273) 730499

While the multi-chambered downstairs bar remains ever popular with Brighton's goths and tattooed, alt-rock musos, the venue upstairs has found its second wind in the last decade. In contrast with the spit-and-sawdust fleapit that is Sticky Mike's Frog Bar (which is *not* a criticism), the Albert has cabaret-style seating (albeit only a handful of tables), a decent PA, charming star-curtain backdrop, a mirrorball and occasional candlelight. The range of nights here is wildly eclectic and often free, so there are few in Brighton whose tastes and pockets are not well served at some point.

The Brighton Dome, Corn Exchange and Studio Theatre

Church Street/New Road (01273) 709709
brightondome.org

After a £22 million refurbishment many years back, which included the installation of a state-of-the-art sound system and new bar area, the Dome returned from the grave offering classical concerts, world music, comedy events and a plethora of big-name artists from Ken Dodd to Sufjan Stevens. Next door the cavernous Corn Exchange offers what is, essentially, a rectangular Dome and has seen the likes of The Go! Team and Grandaddy (RIP) pack the place. Just round the corner from both of these, the Studio Theatre is a much smaller room that features more intimate performances and, whilst generally eschewing 6Music types, is *the* place to catch your favourite Venezuelan elbow-flute player.

Concorde 2
Madeira Drive, Brighton seafront
(01273) 673311
www.concorde2.co.uk

Operating just below the radar of the Dome complex – but still putting on intriguing and up-and-coming acts you actually may have heard of – this is an excellent live venue, even if the view-blocking antique iron posts on the right can mean that you don't see the face of the keyboard player all night. (See also *Discotheques*)

The Green Door Store
(see Discotheques)

The Haunt (see Discotheques)

The Hope and Ruin
11-12 Queens Road (01273) 325793
www.drinkinbrighton.co.uk/hope-and-ruin

Recently renovated downstairs in a bid to make it more 'Brighton' (the arse end of a caravan as the food counter and a scattering of retro furniture) and perhaps to discourage townies looking for their tenth pint at 9pm on their way to West Street. Upstairs is a key venue on the Brighton music scene and sprang from the ashes of the long-defunct Lift Club. On a busy night you'll find 90-odd skinny-trousered types here to see the latest guitar gods and goddesses strutting their stuff. If you prefer your gigs intimate, this is the place to come. We've always held to the notion that the smaller the venue and the cheaper the tickets, the better the gig. Why spend £100 to stand at the back of a football stadium watching a giant plasma screen when you can spend £6 and actually be able to smell the singer's armpits? Come to every single gig they put on and in a few years you'll be able to say: "Aching Testicles' Dreams are playing at the Brighton Centre? Listen mate, I remember seeing them at the Hope. It was only a few quid. And I stood right at the front and got to touch the bassist's kneecap with my pinkie..."

Poor old Banksy gets overwhelmed by rock legends on the side wall of the Albert

LOCAL PROMOTERS

Dictionary Pudding/Riots Not Diets

Tobi, a tall floppy haired lad, puts on shows for bands with funny names (e.g. Lovely Eggs) from the burgeoning underground indie scene. You'll find his gigs at the community run Cowley Club or The Hope and Ruin.

Terrace Cred

Run by husband and wife team Paul and Ashley, these are intimate and high quality nights featuring Americana or singer-songwriters, held in small cosy pubs, especially The Greys on Southover Street. Sometimes they even happen in Paul and Ashley's front room!

One Inch Badge

www.oneinchbadge.com

Probably the largest promoters in Brighton, whose gigs range from 6Music/Vice Magazine type acts through to mainstream hitters. They also run festivals and venues in Brighton.

Melting Vinyl

Contact Anna (01273) 325955
www.meltingvinyl.co.uk, info@meltingvinyl.co.uk

Northern lass Anna 'eh-up' Moulson has been beavering away in Brighton for two decades now as a top promoter, and is responsible for some of the best gigs in town; everything from arty indie pop to twisted electronica comes under her wing. To her credit she arranged the first-ever Brighton shows for The Strokes and White Stripes and has put on gigs by such luminaries as Julian Cope, Emiliana Torrini, Howe Gelb and underground Norwegian one-man band Baconboyfjord. As well as regular gigs at the Green Door Store, The Hope and Ruin and Komedia she has put on events in local churches, and even Fred's old allotment shed in Peacehaven. Support this lovely Yorkshire lady. It would be awfully quiet in Brighton without her.

Eee baa gum, Anna Moulsecoomb looks forward to another groundbreaking promotion

Resident
Kensington Gardens (01273) 606312
www.resident-music.com

The places for tickets, latest releases and general info on who's playing and when. Times have changed from when a hairy bloke would grunt at you from behind the counter when you wanted some advice. Now it feels likes a combination of an independent and a chain, nicely designed and friendly.

Dance 2 Records
129 Western Road (01273) 220023

Tickets for everything related to dance, DJ and club culture, including big festivals and the likes of Beatdown and Devotion.

Dome Box Office
New Road (01273) 709709

For all the bigger events at the Corn Exchange, the Pavilion Theatre and the Dome itself. Also the main ticket office during the Brighton Festival and Fringe.

THE POP CELEBRITY
HALL OF FAME

It is a well-established fact that, apart from Fatboy Slim, everyone in Brighton is a musician of some sort. With a glut of successful acts in recent years from George Ezra to Bat for Lashes, and with the Brighton Institute of Modern Music (BIMM) attracting popstar wannabes from all over the world, it seems only right we celebrate the town's euphonious achievements. Below is a helpful guide to the popstars of past and present who at one time or another have graced our city. We must admit, though, some of it may be based on hearsay and an overactive imagination.

FAMOUS FOR 15 MINUTES

Kirk Brandon (Spear of Destiny, definitely wasn't Boy George's lover, oh no)

Electrelane (now split up sadly, though keep your eyes peeled for a reunion gig in twenty years or so)

Peter and the Test Tube Babies (Still going and still not very famous)

The Piranhas (Ska punk outfit best known for their cover of *Zambesi*)

These Animal Men (*NME* darlings who lived entirely off speed and hair dye)

STILL THROWING TVs OUT OF WINDOWS

Bat for Lashes
British Sea Power
Brakes
Nick Cave
Norman Cook
Dave Clarke
Dave Gilmour
The Electric Soft Parade
Freemasons
Fujiya & Miyagi
Grasscut
Gazelle Twin
The Go! Team
The Kooks
The Levellers
Oddfellow's Casino
Tom Odell
Royal Blood
David Thomas (Pere Ubu)
Tim Bick

{·}·} **Splitting Images**
celebrity lookalike agency

Leo Sayer Lookalike

Keith Thomas

Wonder if he gets a lot of work?

SO YOU WANT TO BE A ROCK AND ROLL STAR?

Brighton Institute of Modern Music (BIMM)
www.bimm.co.uk

So you want to be a rock and roll star? sang cynical Byrds lead singer Jim McGuinn shortly before joining the Subud faith and changing his name to Roger (they insisted his name had to begin with an 'R'; he suggested Rocket, Retro or Ramjet, they suggested he stop being silly and settle on Roger). But we digress. Here at last is a real School of Rock with genuine professionals who can teach you the riff from Stairway to Heaven, show you where to buy patchouli oil, provide training in how to snort cocaine off a dwarf's head and more besides. But we're sure they've heard those gags a thousand times. In truth BIMM is brilliant for budding musicians and anyone serious about learning the ins and outs of this sordid but rewarding profession. Through BIMM you can get a diploma in everything from sound engineering and tour management to songwriting.

Heroes, Eccentrics & Celebrities

Brighton has always attracted more than its fair share of outlandish individuals, and below is a guide to some of the town's fruitiest and most lovable rogues and mavericks. Far from being branded loonies, these individuals are championed here for their style, courage, humour and lust for life. Saying that, does anyone remember the Bread Man, the guy who used to wander the streets of North Laine between six and seven in the morning with two French loaves strapped to his head like helicopter blades? Now he *was* a loony.

Disco Pete

A cross between Bez and your favourite grandad, Disco Pete is a permanent fixture at any outdoor Brighton music event, usually attired in his flame shirt, bangles, beads, hat and Michael Jackson glove. Pushing eighty, Pete is so loved in Brighton that he has a hugely popular fan page on Facebook and came third in a poll by Metro on the seven best reasons to live in Brighton. Look out for him at local music festivals and indeed anywhere the sun is shining and live music is playing.

Michael "Atter∫" Attree

Brighton's favourite dandy, Atters has a penchant for sartorial elegance, the paranormal and scantily-clad showgirls, and can generally be found at local auctions, séances, society dos and the Sussex Fencing Club. In his longstanding editor-at-large role at The Chap magazine he has interviewed the likes of Alan Moore, Patrick Moore, Adam Ant, Terence Stamp, Sir Donald Sinden and Brian Blessed. Interviewing Ken Dodd *"to a satisfactory conclusion, while crapulent on LSD"* was, he claims, one of his greatest (yet most terrifying) recent triumphs. A former Honourable Chairman of Brighton's 2007 World Beard and Moustache Championships, Atters continues to preside over such proceedings having compered the last two British Beard & Moustache Championships, including the 2012 event at the Brighton Dome. While Blighty may have long since reached 'peak beard', 'peak tweed' and indeed, 'peak moustache', for Atters, facial topiary and rakishness remains a way of life.

Chris Macdonald

Chris has spent the past twenty-five years in Brighton constructing beautiful strange sculptures out of wood and found objects in his studio in North Laine. There is something Daliesque about the way he juxtaposes curious metal gadgets (such as old camera parts or giant cogs) with beautifully carved wooden items, but the finished pieces are wholly original, the work of a man who fell down Alice's rabbit hole and never returned.

Chris's sculptures can be purchased from his website or spotted in different shops and galleries around town. And if you want to actually drop in on him for a cuppa and a chat about art, get a copy of *Cheeky Walks in Brighton and Sussex* and take yourself on the Art Trail.

Birdy Man

Birdy Man can be seen wandering through North Laine most weekends when the sun is shining, though to be honest you'll hear him long before you see him. While best known as the nattily attired purveyor of imitation bird whistles, Tim (as he's known to his mum) is also an actor and a demonstration of the lengths people in Brighton will go to avoid getting a proper job. But don't get any funny ideas about copying him. The brief appearance of Butterfly Man on Bond Street a few years back got his pecker up and you can guess who came off the worse.

Lorraine Bowen

Overnight star of *Britain's Got Talent* and The Casio Queen of Brighton, Lorraine is an eccentric songwriter with a massive organ collection in her loft. Such is her mania for 80s organs that the strains of bossa-nova beats can be heard winding their way up around the vicinity of Brighton Station where she resides.

"It's the auto accompaniments I most love," she sighs passionately. *"It's that little piece of musical history that gets me right there!"* pointing to her nether regions! *"Sometimes the dodgy 80s wiring helps to create that little bit more vibrato than you'd expect from an ordinary organ."*

Her collection mainly involves the Casiotone range but her proudest possession is an original brown 1981 Omnichord that Billy Bragg gave her when she was working with him as piano player/vocal coach in the 90s. Lorraine is most famous for her *Crumble Song*, which has now been translated into five languages. She performs round the world and will accept donations of old organs (especially with dodgy wiring).

The Birdlady of St Peters

If you're wandering around town and notice a jabbering flock of several hundred seagulls, endlessly divebombing a shambling woman with gesticulating limbs, don't scamper in to help out – it s just the Birdlady of St Peters, fulfilling her endless quest to ensure the poor birdies don't go hungry. Often accompanied by a supermarket trolley to hold the score or so loaves of bread that are so necessary to keep our unique species of Brighton gull from becoming extinct (they can no longer digest raw fish, having been raised on a diet of doughnuts, candyfloss and used nappies), the Birdlady does the dirty work that the council refuses to contemplate. Her favourite spot seems to be the grass around St Peters Church on Grand Parade but any green space near the seafront will do. Occasionally she fancies a change and you'll see her standing covered in pigeons, looking like a peculiarly ineffective scarecrow.

Dolly Rocket

Describing herself as *"successful at the very arse end of the entertainment industry and proud of it"* singer, club host, burlesque performer and show-off, Dolly Rocket has been wowing Brighton audiences for more than twenty years now, regularly performing at or hosting some of the town's biggest and best party nights.

A champion for the Amazonian woman, she stands some six feet five inches in her heels. This, combined with her larger-than-life character and impressive curves sometimes leads to her mistakenly being called a drag queen, which she is not. She is in fact, *"the kind of woman drag queens are merely emulating."*

A few of Dolly's career highlights include playing a lesbian pimp alongside Steven Berkoff in the British movie *9 Dead Gay Guys,* and appearing as Boob Woman and Lola Lust in *Electric Blue Adult Video Magazine* (numbers 33 and 34 for those who're interested). She has appeared in the National Portrait Gallery, as well as being photographed by the legendary David Bailey, who told her she had *"beautiful blow-job lips"* (she hastens to add that he didn't get to experience them). Anyone who's seen her perform will no doubt agree that Ms Rocket is not just a gay icon but a Brighton treasure and one hell of a woman!

A Spotter's Guide To
BRIGHTON CELEBRITIES

Brighton has long been home to an eclectic bunch of celebrities, from world famous actors to popstars. What better way to spend an afternoon than going all gooey-eyed and weak-kneed at having stumbled across that bloke from The Bill whose name you can't recall, or the bass player from legendary local band Anal Beard?

NICK CAVE

The brooding Australian singer lives in deepest, darkest Kemptown and can be spotted striding around town in an expensive suit and dark glasses, dreaming up a new novel or album themed around murder, sex, violence and getting on a bit.

37 points

DAVE GILMOUR

Hove resident Dave 'David' Gilmour can be spotted in the corner of the Guitar and Amp shop in North Laine, trying out the latest electric guitars and playing the riff from Smoke On The Water for hours on end. Either that or he's out taking his Alsatian for a walk on Hove seafront.

32 points

PEWDIEPIE

Like a teenager on amphetamines, PewDiePie is a YouTube phenomenon attracting zillions of followers for his insightful comments on the latest computer games, such as: 'Shit me, a monster! Gonna zap that fucker!' He can be spotted walking his dog on Hove seafront.

8 points

DAVID WALLIAMS

Walliams is one of several celebs to live in the glamorous 'Millionaires Row', down near the fish market, docks and cement factory bordering Portslade. In summer he can be spotted in his budgie smugglers about to nip over to France to get some fresh croissants. Either that or he'll be out walking his dog on Hove seafront.

29 points

CHRIS EUBANK

Once an easy spot owing to the fact that Chris spent most of his waking hours driving his juggernaut, motorbike or tractor around the Lanes waving at bemused strangers. Since the bankruptcy he's been keeping his head down. Give him time: he'll be back. Probably as the latest face for the *"I relax on the bus"* campaign.

3 points

ZOELLA

Like a teenager on amphetamines, Zoella is a YouTube phenomenon attracting zillions of followers for her insightful comments on how to wear a dress, put on make-up and deal with mental illness, all in digestible five minute clips. Zoella can be spotted out shopping for stuff to blog about. Either that or she'll be out walking her pug on Hove seafront.

9 points

FATBOY SLIM

From Quentin to Norman to Freakpower to Fatboy Slim (and a host of other pseudonyms along the way), local hero Norman Cook is still releasing records, remixing other people's, Djing and doing his best to support Brighton & Hove Albion. He can be spotted at football matches lleading the chanting. Either that or he'll be out with his wife Zoe, walking their dog on Hove seafront.

18 points

ADELE

Look, if you haven't worked it out by now, just go to Hove seafront, it's overrun with celebrities walking their bloody dogs and Adele is no exception.

14 points

If you've been missed out of our *Spotter's Guide* and feel that you ought to be included, please write to us finishing the following sentence:

I think I'm famous enough to be in your guide because.................................

....

Please enclose £10 and a signed photo. If you are Simon Fanshawe or have just been in *Holby City* a few times, this will not be sufficient.

BRIGHTON RIP

As we've been publishing this guide since 1999, we thought it was time to celebrate some of the places and people that have long since shut up shop, gone to meet their maker or, worse, moved to Worthing. Below are a few excerpts from old reviews that will hopefully prompt a few smiles of recognition from some readers, and have others kicking themselves that they didn't come to Brighton earlier.

The Sunday car boot at Brighton Station

One of the strangest stalls is the one selling manky limbs from Victorian dolls. It's always there so logic dictates there must be a regular stream of people who need them. WHO ARE YOU???

(Sent to the Marina to die)

124 Queens Road bookshop

The window display defies explanation and the whole shop looks as if the owner got a huge truck full of books and just emptied them into the shop and said, "*OK, we're open*". In fact he's always reminded us of Michael Caine in *Educating Rita*, after he's had a few. But ask for any title and he'll wander down one of those war-torn corridors, rummage through a pile and somehow find it. Remarkable to behold.

(Now an estate agents with internet café and photocopying service)

DK Rosen Tailoring Church Street

One customer was refused entry to the shop on the grounds that he was wearing the wrong buttons on his shirt, although Mr Rosen did offer to sew on the correct ones if he didn't mind waiting...

(Now empty; Mr Rosen last seen handing out flyers for Pizza Hut in Hove)

Dynamite Boogaloo club night

Two contestants each wear a pair of knickers onto which is attached a parsnip roughly sculpted into the shape of a dildo. A couple of audience members then sit with legs open as goalposts and contestants have to try and knock a potato through the posts using their dildo...

(Now ended)

Cooper's for Haircuts
Baker Street
He's just like any other 203-year-old desert-rat war-veteran barber who charges 100p a haircut, offers an endless stream of invective about anything, and who cuts bits of your hair actually **out of** your head.
(Now a trendy hairdresser's)

Black Chapati restaurant
Preston Circus
Brighton's most pompous restaurateur, Steve Funnell, will regularly lecture diners on what they are eating; if anyone is spotted talking during these sermons he'll ask them to share the joke with the rest of the class or, on occasion, use the C word and throw them out.
(Now working with Gordon Ramsay)

The Cheese Shop
Kensington Gardens
We asked the woman behind the counter how many times a day someone walked in and quoted the Monty Python cheese shop sketch to her and she answered, *"what sketch?"*
(Now a pet shop specialising in parrots)

The Gloucester nightclub
Some nights it's full to capacity, on others there'll just be a few goths sat in the corner eating jelly.
(Now closed)

Joker Basement comedy club
For the joke competition compere Guy Venables dishes out top-quality prizes ranging from hi-fis to Rolex watches, all pilfered by his mate Dodgy Dave. One month a friend of ours won the home phone number of Brian Sewell.
(Dead but not forgotten)

George Hamilton V B&B
Lower Rock Gardens
When the door opened a rather unshaven man emerged smelling of booze.
Us: *Hello.*
Him: *What do you want?*
Us: *I'm writing a guide book on Brighton and...*
Him: *I'm not interested.*
Shuts the door.
The end.
(Last spotted on Britain's Got Talent*)*

Dr Who obsessives
Seb and Dunc
"Women give you a wide berth when they find out what you're into," explained Dunc, *"but they don't know what they're missing. We can be sensitive. I cry sometimes. I mean, have you seen Dr Who and the Green Death?"*
(Both still single)

Brighton in the Movies

Brighton Rock
1947 Dir. John Boulting

Discover a Brighton of Bovril adverts and Brylcreem in this classic Graham Greene story set in the 30s, with plenty of fascinating scenes from the Old Lanes, Queens Road, Grand Hotel and the Palace Pier. Richard Attenborough plays Pinkie Brown, an evil small-time gangster who tries to cover up a murder by marrying a young girl who could give evidence against him. While the ending is far better in the book (aren't they always?) this is a genuinely chilling account of the gangster scene that once flourished in Brighton. If you're a *Doctor Who* fan keep your eyes peeled for a young William Hartnell.

Classic line from the film: *"People don't change; look at me. I'm like one of those sticks of rock. Bite all the way down and you still read Brighton"*.

Oh! What A Lovely War
1969 Dir. Dickie Attenborough

Attenborough's first movie is an over-ambitious and heavy-handed affair, telling the story of the First World War through allegory, satire and *way* too much singing. The West Pier is the platform for events leading up to the war, and the film does include many fine shots of the seafront, the Downs and Devil's Dyke.

Despite its flaws it's an interesting piece of British movie history, with some occasionally stunning moments. The scene in the trenches on Christmas Day, when the German and English soldiers nervously meet in no man's land and share a drink, is genuinely moving. The film also boasts an incredible cast, ranging from thespian gods Laurence Olivier and John Mills to the Fairy Liquid queen, Nanette Newman.

Quadrophenia
1979 Dir. Franc Roddam

Jimmy, a troubled young Mod, visits Brighton for a wild weekend but gets carried away, takes too many pills, loses his job and is so disillusioned with Sting's acting that he drives his scooter off Beachy Head. Or does he?

The shots of 70s Brighton (masquerading as 60s Brighton) are wonderful – it's all smoky cafés, Triumph Heralds and Wimpy bars. The fight scenes take place down East Street and on the beach (where potatoes were substituted for stones!). If you want to find the famous alleyway where Jimmy and Steph cop off, go down East Street toward the sea. Look for the pair of shops called Aston Bourne and between them is a sign for an alleyway that reads 'to little East Street'. It's down there. Yes, the doorway is still there, but it's locked so, no, you can't pop in and have a shag, though countless have tried…

Classic line from the film: "*I don't want to be like everyone else, that's why I'm a Mod see.*"

Down Terrace
2009. Dir. Ben Wheatley

Named after the unpicturesque street in Brighton where it was filmed, this is a blackly comic crime drama where the blackness almost blots out the comedy, wherein a drug dealing family try to pinpoint the police informant in their midst. While lacking the more advanced concepts and budgets of Wheatley's later films, Down Terrace's paranoia and claustrophobic tone still make it an interesting film, though it is not an easy watch - like Shane Meadows' *Dead Man's Shoes*, the violence is highly explicit and the mood disturbing. What is refreshing, given that this must be the thousandth crime movie to be filmed in this town, is that it eschews the recognisable and now clichéd locations of seafront, pier and railway station in favour of the rather less scenic east Brighton area. In fact, the film is so geared towards displaying the unlovely, one scene even features Brighton law courts, a building so gruesomely ugly that it was previously thought to be unfilmable using existing technology.

20,000 Days on Earth

2014 Dir. Iain Forsyth and Jane Pollard

Beautifully filmed and shot in various locations close to his seafront home (some at night) this purports to be a day in the life of musician Nick Cave. But is it? Playfully twisting fact and fiction, the filmmakers delve into his childhood, friendships, collaborations and creative process.

Highlights include seeing Nick and the band creating some of the music for his masterpiece *Push the Sky Away* album, and the powerful countdown right at the beginning of the film. While overly manicured (Cave fails to disclose any vulnerabilities, save for his vanity) this is an inspiring and highly innovative self-portrait of an artis who is still at the peak of his powers.

"There was a young woman from Ealing..."

CARRY ON BRIGHTON

Carry On Girls
1973 Dir. Gerald Thomas

Where in Brighton?

It all takes place in the pretend seaside town of Fircombe (oooerrr!!) which is, of course, actually Brighton. The film features shots of the seafront, the West Pier and a fleeting glimpse of Regency Square. Our favourite bit of the film is near the end, when the contest goes awry and Sid James – chased by a crowd of angry men – escapes down the West Pier in a go-kart. Look out for the outrageous gay stereotypes in the movie – there's the camp film director with the flowery shirt and mincing walk and June Whitfield's sidekick: a humourless, man-hating lesbian who dresses like Hitler. They just don't make comedy clichés like they used to.

The Plot:

Sid James is on the make as usual, this time as the buttock-slapping Councillor Fiddler, who organises a beauty competition only to be foiled by sour-faced women's-libber June Whitfield.

Trivia:

This was the first *Carry On* film that had to be broadcast after the BBC's 9pm watershed, as it was considered far too saucy!

Carry On at Your Convenience
1971 Dir. Gerald Thomas

The Plot:

Hailed as a *Carry On* masterpiece, this tale of industrial strife and romance at WC Boggs toilet factory meant that finally the lavatorial gags could really let rip (ahem). And, of course no *Carry On* movie would be complete without Brighton's own Patsy Rowland (as sex-crazed secretary Miss Withering) trying to get into Kenneth Williams' trousers. We just don't think you were his type, dear. Starring Kenneth Williams as WC Boggs and Sid James as… Sid. Well, why make life difficult?

Where in Brighton?

The gang take a bus trip down for their annual works outing and head for the rides on the Palace Pier.

Trivia:

Alternative title for the film was *Carry On Ladies Please Be Seated*.

The Gay Scene

Since the first gay herring fair in 1910 Brighton's gay scene has grown to become the largest and most celebrated in the country. Gay shenanigans had been going on well before then however – most of the Prince Regent's male friends were camp as Christmas and the Pavilion is a classic example of what can happen when you let a gay man loose on the decorating.

By Victorian times Brighton had become the destination of choice for the London homoset wanting to get away from prying eyes. Oscar Wilde met his lover Bosie in the Albion Hotel while Gladstone even had his own drag show. It is the town's theatrical tradition that really played the biggest role in creating the scene as we know it today; gay icons like Ivor Novello and Noël Coward lived here, lording it up and down with Laurence Olivier with whom, ironically enough, you can now ride up and down the seafront, should you catch the number 27 bus. And of course with the town already established as a fashionable pleasure capital, and with place names such as Dyke Close, The Queen's Arms and Tidy Street, Brighton really was the obvious choice for the UK's gay headquarters.

From the 60s onwards the gay community developed around Kemptown, the Old Steine and St James's Street. You'll find most of the best bars, clubs and shops here as this is where the majority of Brighton's gay population still socialises, although truth is, they are now scattered all over the place: they're everywhere!

The original gay haunts in Kemptown were developed for cruising but as it became so much easier to be 'out' in Brighton, the clubs and bars became less about a quick fumble in the loos and more about just hanging out, posing and socialising (though, believe us, plenty of naughtiness still goes on).

Statistics show that 10% of adults in Brighton are LGBT, with the number still rising. And with the advent of the same sex couples act, Brighton is fast becoming the gay 'wedding' capital of the country, with his-and-his peach Audi TT wedding presents to match. So let's raise a toast and be queer and proud. As Emily Lloyd was so fond of saying in the Brighton-set Wish You Were Here, "up yer bum!"

LOCAL BARS

The Bulldog
31 St James's Street (01273) 696996
www.bulldogbrighton.com

31-hour drinkathons, compulsory happy hours and promotions galore, the Bulldog is somewhere to drink and cruise: a place where nobody wants to know your name but everyone wants to shag you (provided you're not too ugly). Despite a slight increase in popularity with the younger gay crowd, the lecherous old-school vibe is still predominant; it's populated most nights by 'mature' gentlemen, many of whom prefer staring to speaking. Rest assured this is a place where you'll only leave alone if you *really* want to.
Top tip: don't bring your granny.

Camelford Arms
Camelford Street (01273) 622386
camelford-arms.co.uk

A spacious, friendly and welcoming pub in the heart of Kemptown, offering good food and frequented by straight and gay couples, bears and students. It claims to the be 'the most dog friendly pub in town' and on Tuesdays hosts a canine-themed pub quiz just for dogs, with one bark for yes, two barks for no, and three barks for 'can you repeat the question please?' The Camelford really does feel like a pub that's well designed and cared for, with its Moroccan themed 'garden', over the top chandeliers and little details like the snug packed with toys and flags. Top marks all round.

Almost everyone in Brighton is gay these days

Marine Tavern

13 Broad Street. (01273) 681284
marinetavern.co.uk

This tiny little wood panelled bar with its stained glass frontage has barely changed since the days when you had to knock on the door of gay places and say the password to gain entry. And to celebrate that idiom, the Marine holds a once a month 80s style early hours session where you still have to do exactly that. The rest of the time it's a friendly sociable down to earth boozer where you can get a decent pint of Otter, take part in a quiz, scoff a curry, or win the back half of a cow in the meat raffle.

The Marlborough

4 Princes Street (01273) 570028
www.marlboroughtheatre.co.uk

Just off the Old Steine, Brighton's long-established lesbian pub attracts a young crowd of gay women, from the civilised to the downright lairy. There are two bar areas: a lively one – usually occupied by feisty dykes monopolising the pool table – and a quieter one next door which has wooden panelling and leather chairs and feels a bit like a Victorian living room.

The Marlborough is a good place to pick up gay magazines and information and is also reputed to be one of Brighton's most haunted buildings – the ghost of Lucy Packham occasionally appears, gets her boobies out for the girls and then rolls them along the floor just for fun. There's also a gorgeous theatre upstairs, run with passion and zeal, offering a wealth of entertainment, especially during the festival.

The Queen's Arms

7 George Street (01273) 696873
thequeensarms.wix.com/thequeensarms

After decades of monogrammed carpets and framed photos of a Worthing DJ called Bubbles, the Queen's Arms has had a gentrification makeover. And while no-one is going to miss having to endlessly re-watch the old landlord's soft porn pop video that was permanently on a loop, it's hard not to feel that some of the charm is now lost with the uniform high tables and chairs and sober colour scheme. At heart however the Queen's Arms remains *the* hotspot for drag queen entertainment, acerbic wit and the promise of a BJ in the loo from a German tourist. If the shrieking of hen parties sets your teeth on edge, you may prefer to visit during the week.

The Zone

33 St James's Street (01273) 682249

Like the Ranelagh this is another of those slightly surreal St James's anomalies. Walk past here any evening of the week and you'll spy a handful of drunk folk dancing like lunatics to a lesbian country band or belting their way through a camp karaoke classic. But with the decor and feel of the place more akin to a David Lynch film than a classic gay cabaret bar, it's like being part of a bizarre drunken wedding party inside a giant glass bottle. You'll either be irresistibly drawn in and end up dancing with a sixty-year-old man with no teeth and two paralytic girls in their twenties or stagger on by with an air of disbelief.

Haemorrhoid-support team training session

FASHIONABLE BARS

Legends
31-34 Marine Parade (01273) 624462
www.legendsbrighton.com

This expansive and modernised hotel bar is mostly about the sea-facing front terrace and languid sun-kissed posing. Even in winter. A younger and slightly more discerning crowd seem to frequent here than the nearby A-Bar, though compared to places like the Camelford round the corner it still feels rather impersonal. Downstairs their Basement Club has a groovier feel, a good mix of music and punter ages, and best of all they don't even charge for entry. A word of caution: if you're staying in the hotel and value your shuteye, get a room at the back and forgo the seaview – the bar's open till very late.

Charles Street
8 Marine Parade (01273) 624091
www.charles-street.com

For uber-posers, Charles Street should be first port of call as it is *the* place for the early twenties crowd and out-of-towners looking for action. A shedload of cash has been spent making it look like a vast *Star Trek* departure lounge, with a bar stretching to the edge of the galaxy. Should the earbending din become too much for you then you can always nip downstairs to the spacious vestibule outside the loos; you never know, you might see something you like.

CLUBS AND CLUB NIGHTS

Envy @ Charles Street
8 Marine Parade (01273) 624091
www.charles-street.com

Standing upon the hallowed ground that many moons ago was heavy metal Valhalla the Hungry Years. we used to joke about it being appropriated by the gay scene and then, suddenly, it was – bringing a whole new meaning to the phrase *"having studs on your back"*. Popular with students and a younger crowd, this is now a gay clubber's paradise, with visits from big-name London clubs and a cavernous space that makes cruising nice and easy. Expect everything from trashy disco nights to the legendary TV night Transister.

Club Revenge
32-34 Old Steine (01273) 606064
revenge.co.uk

Still the biggest gay club on the south coast, open six nights a week with

special events, drinks promotions, strippers and cheesy pop nights. It's a little on the expensive side but ranks as one of the best in the UK. Sure, newcomers will find the inevitable cliques, but don't be put off: it really isn't difficult to meet new people here. With all those body beautifuls sweating it out on the upstairs dancefloor, you shouldn't find it hard to get caught up in the contagious party atmosphere.

Top tip: be nice to the sexy and flirty barstaff – they are your best port of call to find out everything about the hottest bars and parties. .

SubLine
129 St James's Street (01273) 624100
www.sublinebrighton.co.uk

More hardcore than the other clubs, SubLine is generally dress code-free apart from their specific leather, sportswear or underwear nights. Still no neoprene night though, which seems odd for somewhere in an area so popular for watersports.

Pride: a recipe for excess

Early August   www.brightonpride.co.uk

Take 100,000+ highly-charged gay folk; dress them up in as many feathers, sequins, leather jock straps, masks, ribbons and glitter as you can; stir in every intoxicant known to man; pour on the sunshine; march them up and down the streets of Brighton and finish off in a huge park with dance tents, funfairs and more wildlife and antics in the undergrowth than a BBC nature programme and you're beginning to get an inkling of the utterly fabulous, depraved carnival that is Pride.

From just 103 people at the first angry, political Pride demonstration, this event has grown to become *the* event in the British gay calendar. A week-long arts festival culminates in a huge carnival procession with stunning floats, dancers, drag queens, classic cars and scantily-clad people of all types enveloped by pumping music. The parade starts on the seafront at 11am and then dances, shouts and camps it up all the way to Preston Park, stopping only for a sandwich and a glass of fizzy pop at the Open Market. It's mirrored by the Village Party in Kemptown which seals off the streets for the entire weekend. Bear in mind that both the Park and Village events are no longer free and can sell out so ensure you buy your wristbands in advance. And in 2013 Brighton started the world's first ever Trans Pride, which takes place the weekend before. Pride is simply fantastic, not to be missed.

CRUISING AREAS

Almost the whole of Brighton is a cruising area, so take your pick: Queens Park, Preston Park, Dyke Road Park, Somerfield… just follow your nose and you can't go far wrong (unless you find yourself in Moulsecoomb, in which case – run!) If you want more concentrated trade, the following places might be of interest…

Brighton Nudist Beach
Ten minutes east of Brighton Pier

If it's pervs, pebbles, flabby bottoms, curious bi-boys, randy gay men, a plethora of stiffies, lots of parading and a stray drunken hen party you're after, then get yourself down to the celebrated nudist beach. It's even conveniently close to the bushes should you happen to meet a likeable fellow. Straights are welcome in theory but in most cases will feel uncomfortable, especially if they get asked for a poppers-fuelled hand shandy by a tattooed man with a heavily pierced penis and a parrot on his shoulder.

Duke's Mound
Nine minutes east of Brighton Pier

This small, sloping, dense shrubbery is the oldest cruising ground in Sussex and comes complete with its own little eco-system and constant stream of lusty men. It affords enough privacy to those who require it, yet is risqué enough for naughty exhibitionists, while those splendid chaps from the Terrence Higgins Trust even come here at weekends to give out free condoms, tea, coffee and oranges at half time.

While not commonly reported, there are occasional stories of people getting mugged after being picked up and taken to Duke's Mound, so take care.

Hove Seafront
The Meeting Place café can be a good spot for cruising during the day (though don't get your hopes up on a drizzly February afternoon), while at night the whole area from the Peace Statue to the King Alfred leisure centre can sometimes seem like one long glorious golden mile of talent.

6 Holes For £6

UNDERSTANDING THE LINGO

The old gay dialect Polari was first developed back in the 1930s when homosexuality was still illegal (unless you were involved in theatre, where it was compulsory). This secret language enabled gay folk to get on with matters at hand without fear of persecution. It was later popularised by Julian and Sandy on the radio show Round The Home *and by the 1970s had evolved into such an esoteric and bizarre tongue that Oliver Postgate used it in* The Clangers *to send secret messages to many of his male lovers around the UK.*

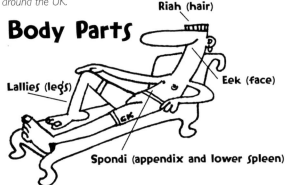

Body Parts

Riah (hair)

Lallies (legs)

Eek (face)

Spondi (appendix and lower spleen)

Bona polone/homi

Dictionary definition - Good looking woman/man
Eg. *That bloke from the* Cheeky Guide, *what a bona homi!*

Chicken

Dictionary definition - Waif-like young man
Eg. *Check out the chicken in Somerfield.*

Cruising

Dictionary definition - Sail to and fro for protection of shipping, making for no particular place or calling at a series of places.
Hmmm, that just doesn't seem to be what's going on in the bushes.

Trade

Dictionary definition - Sex/Your pick-up for the evening
Eg. *Take your trade home and give him something to remember you by.*

Varda/vada

Dictionary definition - To check out
Eg. *Varda the legs on him/her/that lovely Regency sofa.*

Others still in use

Kamp: Effeminate (Known As Male Prostitute)
Naff: Ugly/bad (Not Available For Fucking)
Omi-polone: Gay man
Lallies: Legs
Plate: Feet/to suck off
Scarper: To run off
Sharpy: Police
Troll: Walk about (looking for trade)

Eg.:*"Varda the naff lallies on the omi-polone! I've trolled for trade but it's scarpered 'cos of sharpy."*
Translation: *"Ey-up, looks like another bloody evening at 'ome, tugging me'sen off."*

SHOP

Prowler

112 St James's Street (01273) 683680
Mon-Sat 10.30am-6.30pm, Sun 12noon-6pm
www.prowler.co.uk

Part of a small chain of gay lifestyle shops that includes one in London and Birmingham, Prowler proudly adds a little culture and sophistication to the formula. Catering mostly for the guys, the shop is perhaps best loved for its large selection of gay literature and 'How to' manuals, as well as the cards, toys, mags, DVDs and aussieBum pants. If you're after something a little more saucy, you'll find it hidden away at the back of the shop. The manager explained, *"We want to be inviting to all. We even had a couple of nuns in the other day looking at cards. That's why it's important to us to keep the contents of the Blue Room separate from everything else. It doesn't have to be thrust into people's faces".* Amen.

SAUNAS

Used as social clubs in Brighton by the gay community, these saunas attract a wide age range and all come with rest room facilities.

Brighton Sauna

75 Grand Parade (01273) 689966
www.thebrightonsauna.com

What with dark rooms, sling rooms and glory hole cabins, this place has got the lot (and a sauna). They don't charge for towels, tea or coffee, there's free condoms and lube, and even a discreet smoking area where there's no need to put your clothes back on. Now *that* is luxury. Just be careful where you flick your burning embers.

The Boiler Room Sauna

84 Denmark Villas, Hove (01273) 723733
www.theboilerroomsauna.com

A good-quality sauna, popular with Hove residents. Parties held at weekends. Expect the odd stray blue-rinse granny who's wandered in looking for a perm.

"So that's where you hid the soap!"

BRIGHTON PEERS
by Cool CHEESE
ITALIAN WAITER
LIVES: TINY FLAT IN PRESTON STREET WITH FOUR OTHER WAITERS
SPOTTED: IN OCEANA'S EVERY NIGHT OF THE WEEK
FLIRTS WITH YOUR DATE WHILST HE'S SERVING YOU
WHITE SHIRT THAT'S BEEN THROUGH THE WASH SO MANY TIMES IT'S GONE SEE-THROUGH
TALKS JUST LIKE YOU BUT ADDS AN 'A' AT THE END OF EVERY WORD
OKAY-A?
OLD DISHCLOTH FROM THE KITCHEN
HOLD ON! WHY WOULD YOU WANT PEPPER ON A CHICKEN MADRAS? THIS IS A CURRY HOUSE!!
PEPPERMILL THAT'S HALF THE LENGTH OF THE RESTAURANT
HIPS THAT GRIND IN TIME TO THE PEPPERMILL

Sex, Fetish
& Body Modification

Brighton has long been the archetypal place for fat London bosses with hairy bums to bring their secretaries for more than just a telesales conference. And, being a fashionable resort and the perfect short break from the Big Smoke, it's easy to see why Brighton has earned a reputation for dirty weekends and countless indiscretions. Even the Prince Regent was at it, having secretly married Mrs Fitzherbert here (the passageways connecting his Pavilion bedroom to her place were a means of ensuring their midnight rendezvous were kept secret).

There are even rumours that Brighton has its own dogging scene up at Devil's Dyke, which – if you're unfamiliar with such antics – involves randy couples, cars and the odd voyeur (I'm sure you can piece the rest of the jigsaw together for yourself).

Brighton's saucy nature today comes more from the liberal outlook of its citizens than anything else. It's a good place to live for anyone who wants to come out of the closet and feel relaxed with his or her sexuality. And as this town is home to everyone from fetishists to drag queens, you can feel secure in the knowledge that, in your very neighbourhood, there'll always be someone kinkier than you.

She Said

32 Ship Street. (01273) 777811
Mon-Sat 10am-6pm, Sun 11.30am-5pm
www.shesaidboutique.com

The creation of Nic Ramsey, She Said offers alluring and exotic lingerie, superior quality toys, sexy knickers, stockings and a large range of corsets. Their new Ship Street premises draws the line as before; the ground floor is an elegant boudoir dressing room, and the stairs take you to a fine selection of dildos, the Alan Titchmarsh-endorsed We Vibe, floggers (from horsehair whips to bejewelled crops), restraints, collars and antique cast-iron nipple clamps. It is the elegant touches, though, that make She Said the Marilyn Monroe to Ann Summers' Miley Cyrus – the decor is beautiful and stylish and the staff, too, dress to impress. A kinky and mischievous version of the shop that Mr Benn used for his psychedelic travels (though where he'd have ended up dressed in exotic underwear and a corset is anybody's guess), with its sassy staff and elegant layout, She Said must lay claim to being one of the most glamorous boutiques in England.

Taboo

2 Surrey Street (01273) 263565
Mon-Sat 9am-8pm, Sun 11am-6pm,
www.tabooshop.com

Leave the furry handcuffs behind and enjoy a sex shop that sells the real McCoy. Taboo stocks quality bondage equipment, the best selection of latex and PVC clothes in the city, a good range of sex toys, fetish books and magazines, and an entire room full of DVDs that vary from straight porn to girl-on-goat action.

In addition to being a good spot for finding out about local fetish nights, sex clubs and other kinky events, this is where you're likely to find some of the more outré devices that might otherwise entail a visit to Antwerp and an encounter with a man wearing a rubber pig's head.

It's no surprise that past accolades include Sex Shop of the Year. Highly recommended for those looking for quality over quantity.

SEX, FETISH & BODY MODIFICATION

Lust

43 Gardner Street (01273) 699344
Sun-Fri 11am-6pm, Sat 10.30am-7pm
www.lust.co.uk

Located in the heart of North Laine amongst trendy boutiques and eateries, Lust lures you in with a curious semi-innocent window display that combines novelty toast racks with mannequins dressed as wet-dream policewomen. . Once inside the funky gifts and quirky homeware initially take centre stage, with just the occasional tub of lube to hint that the back room and other two floors are considerably saucier. While their companion shop Taboo is stocked more for professional fetishists and porn-lovers, Lust offers a wider range of stock from games, books and playthings for the cheeky stag / hen parties to sex toys, beginners' S&M kits, bondage equipment and strap-ons. There's a modest collection of PVC, rubber and uniforms aimed at those dipping their toes for the first time into the world of kinky glamour-wear.

Like Taboo, everything is well displayed, the dressing room suitably seductive and staff well-informed and eager to please. At last, a sex shop for the twenty first century.

Brighton Body Casting

Hove Enterprise Centre,
Unit 6 Basin Road North, Hove
By appt only 07961 338045
Prices from £35
www.brightonbodycasting.com

Established by sculptor Jamie McCartney, Brighton Body Casting offers a highly unusual service: that of turning any body part into a piece of art. From torsos and faces to pregnant bellies and babies' hands, you name it, Jamie has cast it. He's even done a death mask so it's a cradle to grave service! Celebrity parts he's had his hands on include Jackie Chan's face, Trinny and Susannah's bums and Lisa Rogers' foofoo.

Since taking the plunge ourselves with a personal part, we can vouch for Jamie's good humour, conviviality and erm... hands-on approach. The process is in fact, relatively simple: the part in question is covered with blue goo (as used by dentists for casting teeth) which sets into a flexible rubber within two minutes. The cast is then lovingly hand-made in your desired material – anything from plaster to bronze, glass or solid gold. Even rubber is an option, leaving you to do with it as you please.

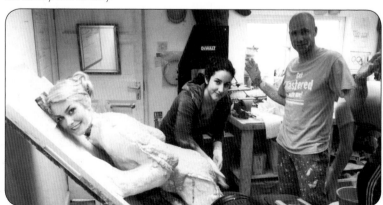

VOTED THE UK'S BEST ADULT SHOP
ADULT TOYS ☆ EROTIC CLOTHING ☆ DVDS

TATTOOS & PIERCINGS

The following studios are only a small selection of what's on offer but are recommended because they take the art of body modification seriously.

While tattooing is a widespread skill, bear in mind that design and style are very individual. If you are tempted, we'd recommend you make an appointment first with the artists below. Go in person to see if you feel comfortable with them and what you think of their work. All good tattooists should carry a portfolio.

One last thing – if you're having something written, make sure your tattooist is clear on the spelling. One local tattoo parlour, which shall remain nameless, used to have a big sign outside that read: "Come inside, we have 1000's of desings". *Enough said.*

Angelic Hell

2 North Road (01273) 697681
Mon-Sat 11am-6pm, Sun 12noon-5pm
www.angelichelltattoo.com

One of the best established tattoo purveyors in town, having notched up nine years of etching the likes of the Brighton & Hove Albion team and one of the Kooks. They've even put Steven Hawking's face on someone's leg, which has already carried off a couple of trophies – the tattoo that is, not the leg*. If you're the sort who acts on impulse you'll be pleased to know that they do walk-ins as well as appointments, plus there's a massive picture window through which your friends can wince and watch the work in progress (there's also a blind that can be drawn if you're shy).

Into You Tattoo

Into You Tattoo

4 Little East Street (01273) 710730
Mon-Sat 11am-6pm
www.into-you.co.uk

When the most renowned tattoo studio in the country opened here in June 2005, it finally nailed Brighton as *the* tattooing centre of England (and quite right too, seeing as we are also the most tattooed population in the UK).

Boasting the internationally famous Alex Binnie and Jason Mosseri among its artists, Into You has an undisputed reputation, particularly for large-scale custom work and hand-done (no gun) tattoos from specialists like Adam Sage. As well as tattoos, they sell tattoo-related jewellery, books, clothes. Of course, quality doesn't come cheap – prices for tattoos start at £50 for a simple name while hourly rates here are £70. But for something as permanent as a tattoo, why settle for anything less than the best?

Nine

9 Boyces Street (01273) 208844
Tues-Sat 11am-6pm,
www.nineboycesstreet.com

Formerly Temple Tatu, now Nine, and shortly to be renamed yet again as Dead Slow, this impressive tattoo studio is located just off West Street, and owners Jack and Kirsty come with years of experience and a deep knowledge and understanding of the history of tattooing.

Newcomers are made to feel at ease by discussing all the processes involved over a cup of tea and the reception room, decorated with artwork by the resident tattooists, is elegant and inviting. Their portfolios

*Isn't it only right that Stephen Hawking responds in kind by having someone's leg tattooed on his face?

are varied and they're particular about researching every design, so you can even find out what the tattoo you're about to get really means.

Top tip: appointments essential.

Punktured

35 Gardner Street (01273) 688144
Mon-Fri 10.30am-6pm, Sat 10am-6pm,
Sun 12noon-5pm
www.punktured.co.uk

Bringing a friendly, open and caring approach to a profession which still has an image of domination by gloomy monosyllabic hairy types, owner Julie and the gang demonstrate their skill and dedication through little touches such as their range of aftercare solutions and written instructions following all piercings, and training all staff in first aid in case anyone feels a bit wobbly afterwards. Not averse to a bit of publicity, Punktured have been featured on TV and radio, were the first piercers to pierce at the London Tattoo Convention and Julie even played Bjork's body double in the Pagan Poetry video. There's plenty on offer including ear scalpelling, dermal anchors, a huge range of body jewellery and even ear piercing (though their oddest request has to be from the woman who brought in her false nipple to be pierced).

Cheeky tip: check their social media for offers and competitions.

Tattoo & Co

6 Kensington Gardens (through the shop below) (01273) 682020
Mon-Sat 10:30am-6pm Sun 11am-5pm

Leaving aside the fact that they obviously don't know what "and company" means, this is a nice little tattoo parlour specialising in old-school designs. Long-term resident artist Alex Newey has now been joined by Fede Borgia, and both offer walk-ins as well as appointments. Meanwhile Danny will pierce literally any part of you (honestly, he offers an extensive list, and *"if it's not on the list I've just missed it out"*). Do note that they share a very small set of rooms with the Velvet Nails salon – when you emerge at the top of stairs into a very pink room you haven't taken a wrong turn.

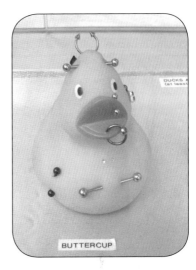

BUTTERCUP

SEX PARTIES

The best place to find out about swingers parties and the like is, inevitably, the Internet. Events like Club Naughtiness happen at SubLine off St James's Street and there are more permanent seven day a week haunts such as Club 77. They welcome couples, go nuts for single women and try and put off any poor single males who happen to be past their prime, sport ponytails or wear socks and sandals.

FETISH CLUBS

Dungeon Bar
12a Regency Square (basement via outdoor steps) (01273) 781220
Fri-Sat 7pm-2am, other occasional nights
www.dungeonbarbrighton.co.uk

Even a saucy fetish bar that we, um we mean, er, a friend visited in Antwerp didn't go quite as far as this place. The Belgians kept the bar and playroom as discreetly door-divided areas, whereas the Dungeon Bar lives up to its name by being exactly that; the equipment is all over this single room bar (and the bar's in a basement handily), so much so that punters can sit round a drinks table that is actually a rubber-lined coffin that may well contain a thirsty submissive. As well as being extremely comprehensive in range, the gear in here is pretty high grade stuff, so as long as you've been properly strapped in by a caring

dominatrix there's no worries about crashing through the window as you're flung from their gigantic rotating wheel. The ever-smiley Kitten Skye keeps this place humming with various special nights from rope classes to more anything-goes events – most fetishes are catered for in some fashion or other. If you're just dipping your toe, the customers are a friendly approachable crowd, it's very female-friendly and mostly chat and imbibing during the early part of the evening as the more hardcore scenesters show up after 10pm. A long overdue addition to Brighton's often hidden world of kink.

ClubSpank
www.spankbrighton.co.uk
From the organisers of the annual Brighton Fetish weekend, this established kinky night is often held in a sports clubhouse. So if you fancy kicking some balls about this is the event for you.

LAPDANCING CLUBS

The Pussycat Club
75 Grand Parade (01273) 689503
www.pussycatclub.co.uk

Grace of Brighton
51-52 North Street (01273) 733212
graceofbrighton.com

Attracting stag nights, rugby teams and visiting businessmen by the coachload, these clubs offer a chance to enjoy lapdances, poledances, VIP dances (behind a curtain), and a range of overpriced drinks. If you don't know the law, strictly no physical contact is allowed between customer and dancer but popping to the loo afterwards to give yourself a hand shandy *is* permitted.

Dungeon Bar

A FETISH PRIVATE MEMBERS BAR

WWW.DUNGEONBARBRIGHTON.CO.UK
INFO@DUNGEONBARBRIGHTON.CO.UK

BRIGHTON PEERS

by Cool CHEESE

YOGA MUM

LIVES:- IN A BASEMENT FLAT IN HOVE WITH HER TEEN-AGE SON AND FOUR CATS

SPOTTED:- CRUISING AT INFINITY FOODS AND AT EVERY YOGA CLASS IN TOWN

BEETROOT COLOURED HAIR AND CHEEKS

CIRCLES UNDER EYES FROM TWENTY YEAR 'ROLL-UP' HABIT

FOUR GALLON BOTTLE OF WATER WHICH SHE CONSTANTLY SUPS ON

PURPLE UNITARD (COVERED IN CAT HAIR)

WORLD'S SMALLEST CRYSTAL

'FREE-RANGE' YOGA MAT

DOING HER PELVIC FLOOR EXERCISES AS SHE CHATS TO YOU ABOUT THE LATEST RETREAT SHE'S BEEN ON IN CLEETHORPES

COPPER BRACELET THAT SAYS SHE'S LACTOSE, GLUTEN AND G.M. INTOLERANT (BUT SHE'S FINE WITH RED WINE AND CHOCOLATE)

Mind Body Spirit

From Yoga and Tai Chi classes to Buddhist centres and homeopaths, Brighton has the lot. Look in the corner of every park and you'll find someone practicing Qi Gong, meditating, doing yoga or (more typically for Brighton) reading about it. Sure, there's the usual mystical crap and places where your cat can have its aura cleansed, but if people believe in it, what's the harm? We love the fact that Brighton people are, on the whole, tolerant and open-minded. After all, why shouldn't you enjoy meditating and chanting as well as, say, clubbing, carpentry and fisting?

SHOPPING

Bell, Book & Candle

23 Gardner Street (01273) 697555
Mon-Sat 10.30am-5.30pm, Sun 11am-5pm

You'll find the classic selection of spiritual cards, books, candles and models of your favourite deity here, as well as more unusual items including a book of spells to entrap prospective lovers, Hindu figurines made from River Ganges mud and plenty of Jewish accessories such as riddush cups, Torah scrolls and gefilte fishfingers.

Two Feathers

11 Kensington Gardens (01273) 692929
Open daily 10am-6pm
www.twofeathers.co.uk

For too long Brighton has suffered under the oppressive yoke of Eastern mysticism, so why not try some Western mysticism from the Navajo Indians? Here's a shop stuffed full of all the tools your friendly neighbourhood shaman needs to get the job done, including carved animal totems, kachina dolls and rattles for shaking at evil spirits, and even bows and arrows for when they absolutely refuse to lay down. They also have a dizzying array of herbs both smokable and brewable (we're not sure exactly what they do but don't blame us if you wake up thinking you're a bald eagle and try to fly out the window) and a Native American fashion range that's most definitely not for vegetarians – cow hide and big chunks of bone rule the day. At the back of the shop there's a calming contemplation pool to stare into, which might come in handy on a Saturday morning when you need to escape the crush of North Laine shoppers. Those who despair about the disappearance of the pre-gentrified Brighton should take heart from the continued existence of this shop in an area of Brighton than is increasingly more about fudge shops and faux-vintage clothes than eccentric shopkeepers and electrical spare parts.

Neal's Yard

2a Kensington Gardens (01273) 601464
Mon-Sat 9.30am-5.30pm, Sun 11am-5pm
www.nealsyardremedies.com

A franchise of one of London's original herbal emporiums, this place has become Brighton's de facto alternative doctor's surgery. With a veritable armoury of herbs, oils, tinctures, vitamins and homeopathic remedies, Neal's Yard also has at its disposal some very clued-up staff (all naturopaths, homeopaths and herbalists) who can help you make informed choices about what you might need. Self-help books are also on hand, as are all the obligatory pampering products should you be suffering from nothing more than a prolonged bout of self-indulgent whinnying. The most usual complaints they deal with are still colds and hay fever but once some guy came in for herbal hormone replacements for his dog. Typical Brighton.

"I assume your goat's a Capricorn?"

THERAPY & BODYWORK CENTRES

Brighton Buddhist Centre
17 Tichborne Street (01273) 772090
Weekdays 12.30-2.30pm for visitors
www.brightonbuddhistcentre.co.uk

Part of The Friends of the Western Buddhist Order, this centre has two stunning meditation and yoga rooms and a library. The Order members wear strange little white collars, are very friendly (try asking *"how will I know when I've reached enlightenment?"* and marvel at their patient response) and make a decent cup of tea. Look out for more unusual stuff going on here too, like theatre and lectures. We went to a great talk during the May Festival one year where a Buddhist theatre director talked about the genius of Tommy Cooper and Frankie Howerd. Sunday school was never like this.

Messianic condensation therapy bags: the latest must-have treatment in Brighton

Cocoon

20-22 Gloucester Place (01273) 686882
Mon-Sat 7.30am-9pm, Sun 9am-5pm
Floating from £25 for 90 minutes
www.cocoonhealthcare.co.uk

If you fancy floating on your back in calm ripple-free salty water under a starlit sky, you've got two options; empty a van-full of Saxa into a duckpond and hope the mallard don't wake up and try to have their way with you, or book into Cocoon's tranquil floatation chamber, which is a bit like a giant shower cubicle with twinkly lights in the ceiling. Or if you're less prone to claustrophobia, choose the pod, which seals you into a big salty sarcophagus. This brand new centre for all things alternative (they also run yoga classes and perform pretty much every therapy you can think of) has been built with great care and taste by owner Emma, so instead of the old Brighton aesthetic of changing room hooks and the odour of sweaty feet, you get soothing white rooms (two for treatments, two for floating, one for massage) with gold basins and relaxing lighting, while sitar music twangs gently away in the background. There's even a Buddha toilet lid in the bathroom, which no doubt assists with a tranquil movement.

The Float Spa

Basement 8, Third Avenue, Hove
(01273) 933680
Mon-Sat 10am-7pm, Sat 10am-5:30pm,
Sun 11:30am-4pm
£65 for an hour's floating, yoga and pilates
www.thefloatspa.co.uk

This spa's 8ft-long 'I-Sopod' tanks bear more than a passing resemblance to sci-fi suspended animation chambers, complete with glowing UV lights and hermetically sealed hatch doors.

However, the floatation therapy is much more primal than it is space-age. The feeling of weightlessness from the Epsom salt in the water, coupled with the total lack of any noise or distraction, provides a short-cut to a deep meditative state. As well as being incredibly relaxing, floating apparently stimulates you intellectually, cures just about every addiction and ailment, and makes your skin nice and soft to boot.

Besides floating, the spa offers a variety of yoga, pilates and meditation classes, as well as courses in everything from mindfulness, hypnotherapy and life-coaching.

Revitalise

86 Church Road, Hove (01273) 738389
123a Western Road. (01273) 710855
www.revitalise-u.co.uk

Previously the hippy-dippy Planet Janet and now rebranded in a twenty first century manner, there's a shop on the ground floor selling organic food products, pills containing your choice of metals and yoga accessories such as Grippa skullcaps for ultra-safe headstands, plus nine consulting and group rooms. Depending on who is renting which, you will generally find an entertaining cocktail of Chinese kickboxing, oneness meditations, chakra dancing classes, tai chi and astrological counselling. Brighton now has its own branch on Western Road, which is pretty much the same deal minus the shop. Be aware that while they do vet the therapists and trainers who use their rooms, they do not employ them, so if you're unhappy with the way your colonic nozzle was inserted you'll need to take it up directly with the person who popped it in.

Samurai Centre/Ninja Shop

49 New England Street/69 North Road
(01273) 570940
www.samuraibrighton.com

The Ninja shop on North Road is *the* place to pick up those stray weapons on your shopping list like swords, staffs, whip chains and nunchaku, while the newly transferred New England martial arts centre focuses on jujutsu and the art of the ninja. Done up to resemble a traditional Japanese dojo, its padded floor makes injuring yourself difficult; disappointingly they've never had any serious sword wounds occur, although they claim mysteriously, *"we do have the means to deal with it"*. If you fancy turning your adorable five-year-old into a trained killer they also run mini-ninja classes.

The Treatment Rooms

21 New Road (01273) 818444
www.thetreatmentrooms.co.uk

There's an element of the geisha about this gorgeously decorated salon, where you feel the only ugly people allowed on the premises are the customers. Massages, body wraps and facials are the main items on the menu here, and for premium prices you get premium pampering: fresh robe and fluffy slippers, your feet gently washed in candle-lit rooms with soothing music, a post-treatment relaxation area with Moroccan recliners, and a glass of herbal tea. You'll walk out of here feeling as light as your wallet, but delighted to be alive.

Unit 4

20-26 Roundhill Street
www.unit4brighton.co.uk

Perched serenely above The Level on the summit of Roundhill is this centre of yogic excellence. Started up by Brighton's legendary yoga guru and Kinks fanatic Pete Blackaby, it is almost entirely devoted to yoga of the Scaravelli style, along with more specialist stuff such as yoga for pregnancy, McTimoney and Feldenkrais.

LAUGHTER CLUBS

Brighton Laughter Club

07891 399 580
emmahiwaizi@gmail.com
www.brightonlaughterclub.org

Founded in 2011, this weekly meet-up group offers laughter sessions based on laughter yoga: a combination of breathing techniques, postures, singing, games and really good knock-knock jokes. Sure, the idea of making eye contact with strangers and pretending to laugh may have some people running for the door; for others it may be just the medicine needed to shake off the blues.

205

What's On

DIARY OF EVENTS

Isn't it only right that the town that likes to party should be host to the biggest arts festival in England? Not only that but throughout the year Brighton plays host to food, film and comedy festivals, car rallies, bike rides, Pride, Burning The Clocks, several music festivals and a firework display every two weeks or so. And with numerous political party conferences, where else could you combine a lovely seafront environment with the sport of egg throwing?

Brighton Science Festival
February
brightonscience.com

This festival, the brainchild of author Richard Robinson, has scientists teaming up with local schools, venues and museums for open days, live experiments, talks and more. You can also catch them letting their hair down at local spoken word nights Café Scientifique and Catalyst Club, where lively late-night debates inevitably turn into a drunken brawl and topless dancing.

The Brighton Festival and Brighton Festival Fringe

May

brightonfestival.org
brightonfringe.org

In May Brighton goes bananas. For three to four weeks the whole town is packed with comedians, novelists, opera singers, dancers, circus acts, street performers, artists, musicians and theatre makers. This is now the third largest arts festival in the world, bringing performers from as far afield as Peru, China and New Zealand, and audiences from as far afield as Hollingbury. If you want to see the town at its most vibrant and colourful, this is the time to visit.

Alongside the main festival runs the Brighton Fringe offering homespun and contemporary performances at more affordable prices in a plethora of venues, theatres and pubs.

An important part of the Fringe is the Open Houses, where artists all over Brighton and surrounding areas open their homes for several weekends and you get a chance to nosey around other people's houses, get a few ideas for your new kitchen and pretend to be there for the art.

During Brighton Festival you can expect everything from guided tours of old cash-machine sites to theatre shows inside the seafront toilets and that bloke on a trapeze wire playing the violin. Over 1000 events, two festivals rolled into one, and the inevitable free fireworks party. Unmissable.

The Great Escape
Weekend mid May
escapegreat.com

*'And lo, for three days and nights
God did smite Brighton with a
plague of shy indie kids with dyed
black hair and skinny-leg jeans
who did impose on the good folk
of the city and say things like,
"Excuse me, I'm trying to get
to see Duh, Yeah? play at The
Haunt but I've lost my phone
and don't know how to use a
map," Or, "Help, I seem to be
trapped inside my trousers, would
someone call my mum?"*

*And the good folk of Brighton
were mildly afraid, but only
because it reminded most of
them that they weren't teenagers
any more and they still secretly
listened to the Levellers.'*

Genesis, chapter four, second
verse (same as the first)

Three manic (and brilliant) days of
gigs all over the city from the latest
asymmetrically haired upstarts and a
few older acts that still hardly anyone's
heard of. If you've not got a VIP pass,
be prepared to stand in some long
queues outside venues. And if you
have got a VIP pass, be prepared to
stand in some medium length queues.

Pride
Early August (See Gay chapter)

Brighton Comedy Festival and Comedy Fringe
October
brightoncomedyfestival.com
brightoncomedyfringe.co.uk

Every October the big names in
comedy descend upon Brighton and
perform their latest shows over an
intensive fortnight at the Brighton
Dome and Corn Exchange. Be warned
though, ticket prices can be no
laughing matter, reaching £25 for just an
hour's stand-up.

For those who prefer to check out
the rising stars of the comedy scene
and save their pennies, look no further
than the Comedy Fringe, set up in
2006 by the good folks at Otherplace
Productions. These guys have their
finger on the pulse of new comedy, and
with tickets at less than half the price of
those in the main festival you'd be a silly
bugger not to give it a try.

Lewes Fireworks
5 November
www.lewesbonfirecouncil.org.uk

Still upset about a bunch of Protestant
martyrs who were burned here
centuries ago by the wicked Catholics,
the people of Lewes remember the
occasion by hosting the biggest and
most phenomenal Bonfire Night
celebration in the UK.

Along with the procession of
carnival-style floats, you'll get the chance
to see the townsfolk dressed up in
Freddy Krueger jumpers, marching
down the streets holding flaming
crosses and throwing bangers (the
exploding variety, not Cumberland).
Around 8pm, the crowds head off

"If we hear anyone shout 'Where's Wally?' again we're going to set fire to them."

to bonfires in different corners of the town where, some years, loonies dressed as cardinals stand on scaffolding and encourage the audience to hurl abuse (and fireworks) at them. A few effigies of the Pope, political figures and crappy celebs are then ceremoniously blown up for good measure, followed by huge firework displays.

The whole event has a very dark, anarchic, pagan feel to it; there are definite hints of The Wicker Man in there. While it's only a short train ride from Brighton we recommend getting there no later than 6pm if you want a good view.

Top tip: waiting to get the train home after the fireworks can be long and gruelling. Best make for the station once the fireworks have begun; you can still enjoy them as you leg it for the train.

Even topper tip: many of the bonfire societies charge for entry to the firework displays these days so it's a good idea to find out the where and what in advance via the website above, or else find yourself watching a couple of rockets over a very distant fence.

London to Brighton Veteran Car Run

First Sunday in November
www.veterancarrun.com

Not being petrolheads we find it hard to join in the excitement of the enthusiasts who congregate down at Madeira Drive, share notes on the pros and cons of tungsten-drive camshafts and then disappear back to their stately mansions. But, as one of our friends put it, "surely the sight of a lot of lovely old cars putt-putting away stirs the little boy in you?"

Cinecity: Brighton Film Festival

November
www.cine-city.co.uk

The city's annual celebration of celluloid, Cinecity was established in 2003 and presents a packed programme highlighting the best cinema from around the world. The festival's home is of course the Duke of York's, but Cinecity screens in all the city's cinemas and in a range of unusual locations – whether it's projections onto the Pavilion or in the cells of the old police station. Past events with a Brighton flavour include local resident Nick Cave selecting his favourite Berlin-set films, and a 25th anniversary screening of cult classic Quadrophenia, with the cast and crew given a Vespa escort to the Grand.

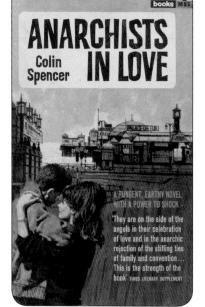

Burning The Clocks

Winter Solstice (around December 22nd)
www.samesky.co.uk

While most seaside towns go into hibernation for the winter, Brighton celebrates the shortest day with this fantastic procession to the seafront, culminating in a huge bonfire and fireworks display. Expect hundreds of strange and beautifully designed paper lanterns around the theme of time, and lots and lots of candles. The whole event evokes that perfect, dark wintry spirit, mixed with the excitement of knowing that Christmas is just around the corner. One of our favourite events in the Brighton calendar. Highly recommended.

Christmas Day Swim

11am Christmas Day
(see Brighton Swimming Club in *The Sea* chapter)

SILAGE

A daring new dining experience

No need for plates or bowls
All food is eaten straight off the table

No need for fancy cups or glasses
Drinks are served in old paint tins

No need for chairs
Meals are best digested when squatting

No need for cutlery
Bring your own hands

All wines locally sourced
From our local off-licence, *Wine Me Up*

SAMPLE MENU

Sprouting potato, herring gull breast, rhododendron sauce
Heritage tomato, nougat, south downs lamb pelt
Black olive ice cream, saveloy jus, fried battenberg cake

Places to Sleep

Brighton has hundreds of places to sleep, from hotels, B&Bs, guesthouses, hostels and hotels to that old mod favourite – under the pier in a sleeping bag. And with such themed places as Drakes, the Pelirocco and Blanch House, some visitors can even expect to find their room decorated by their favourite bands or dressed up as a Moroccan harem. Despite such myriad choices and the proliferation of rooms on Airnbnb , those on a budget may still struggle to find anything both inexpensive and fit for human habitation. So, in our efforts to bring you a flavour of what's out there, we've tried to cover a range from the priciest to the cheapest, the friendliest to the rudest, and the simplest to the most outrageous. A word or two of warning though: booking only one night at weekends can be next to impossible, and Brighton is a noisy place for most of the night so for heaven's sake bring some earplugs.

DEAD POSH

The Grand

Kings Road, Brighton seafront
(01273) 224684
Singles from £100, doubles from £130
www.grandbrighton.co.uk

The most famous hotel in Brighton and, at £500 a night for the King suite, probably the most expensive. Sadly, despite the opulence of the lobby and the doorman standing outside in a big hat, much of the Grand's appeal relies on its history and reputation. From the rusted façade to the tired bedrooms, most of this hotel could do with some serious TLC. All inland rooms face air con machinery (insulting given that most rooms don't yet feature it), and you can expect to pay at least £160 for a sea view. Even if you fork out for a double, it may turn out to be two single beds pushed together.

However, some Grand elements do remain. It is still one of the only hotels to offer valet parking, though this does set you back £30 a day. The spa and treatment rooms are newly refurbished and offer ridiculously decadent services, like champagne and caviar facials.

Dress code: Armani, Nicole Farhi etc. Although if you're just popping in for tea they don't care if you're wearing trackie bottoms and a vest.

Hilton Brighton Metropole

Kings Road, Brighton seafront
(01273) 775432
Rooms £80-180 without meals,
suites £220-280
www.hilton.com

Another famous hotel which seems to be resting on its laurels. The building itself is gorgeous, and well located along the seafront. The lobby area looks impressive, if slightly outdated, with sweeping staircases and chandeliers. However, most of the rooms don't live up to this initial impression. Although half of the hotel has been refurbished, even these updated rooms can suffer from maintenance issues, and the free Internet service is patchy at best — considered as basic a human right as running water nowadays.

While we really can't recommend staying at this hotel we can however,

recommend spending an amusing hour or so reading their Tripadvisor reviews, which include such gems as an anecdote about the bartenders running out of olives for Martinis and using herbed olives from the kitchen instead.

Drakes

43-44 Marine Parade (01273) 696934
Doubles £120-360
www.drakesofbrighton.com

If you fancy soaping your rude bits while enjoying one of the best sea views in Brighton, the majority of the rooms in this sexy and sumptuously designed twenty-room hotel actually come with a freestanding bath in the bedroom, right in front of the window (if you're on the right floor you can wave your loofah at top-deck bus passengers). The pampering extends to wet rooms with gigantic showerheads and under-floor heating, electrically driven curtains that hide wardrobe and desk space, and recycled bamboo-board floors, with air con, internet and mega TV as standard.

Downstairs there's a restaurant and a groovy private bar that never closes, serving the hotel's own custom-

designed cocktails. Despite the glorious luxury and breathtaking rooms, Drakes believe their defining style is service: they'll prepare your room any old way you like, so it can be ready on your arrival with a hot bath drawn, *Carry on Columbus* playing on the TV, balloons, champagne or even a special 'love hamper' from She Said erotic boutique. You don't even have to leave the room to get a haircut. Anything is possible apparently, *"as long as it's legal"*. Recommended.

Hotel Du Vin

2 Ship Street 08447 364251
Doubles from £180-£280, all rooms en-suite.
www.hotelduvin.com

Stunning design, beautiful rooms, friendly staff: Hotel Du Vin just oozes style. The rooms are named after famous wine houses and some include dual-pedestal baths where you and your lover can get up to all sorts of adventures.

There are 37 bedrooms in total, thoroughly modern if not quite as large as you might expect for the price, and a fabulous carved staircase; if you come to visit, keep your eyes peeled for the gargoyles.

The restaurant is now a long way from its heyday but in this location you're surrounded by great places to eat so there's no danger of starvation.

Hotel Una

55/56 Regency Square (01273) 820464
www.hotel-una.co.uk

This hotel manages to be incredibly luxurious but without a hint of pretentiousness. This is no doubt due to the extremely friendly staff, who not only provide brilliant service but are happy just to have a chat. All rooms have a chic and modern air, but the use of light wood and soft brown leather make them feel warm and comfortable too. Our only qualm is the use of string curtains in some rooms and in the lounge area, which seem oddly out of place, not to mention entirely pointless.

Una is ideal for special occasions and romantic getaways. Depending on the occasion your room can be decorated with rose petals or balloons, and with champagne or a birthday cake ready for your arrival. Two of the bedrooms have their own private jacuzzis and sauna rooms if you want to (literally) splash out, and many others have roll-top baths overlooking Regency Square. The higher end rooms even receive a breakfast in bed service.

Finally, their 'Bar55' is ridiculously well-stocked, including barrel-aged Negroni and absinthe-soaked plums, and will have gadget-lovers frothing at the mouth over its magnetic stirrer.

QUITE POSH WITH A HINT OF BOHEMIAN

Amherst

2 Lower Rock Gardens (01273) 670131
Singles £65-120, doubles £75-130,
cooked breakfast £6 extra
www.amhersthotel.co.uk

Amherst pride themselves on making their guests feel special. All the rooms are tasteful and modern while little touches like offering breakfast in bed, free snacks, herbal teas and broadband data points in every room show that lots of thought has gone into the place. And being located very close to the seafront, several of the rooms here have terrific sea views. What more could you ask for? A foot massage while you tuck into your bacon? If you ask nicely they'll probably do that for you too.

Brighton Pavilions Hotel

7 Charlotte Street, Kemptown
(01273) 621750
Singles start at £45, doubles £85-120,
£100-160 for a four poster
www.brightonpavilions.com

Under new management since 2014, the Pavilions has maintained its excellent service (and remarkable cleanliness). Friendly new owners Peter and Steve have redecorated, maintaining some of the chintz but also giving the whole building a modern update. The popular Titanic, Pompeii and Safari-themed rooms will remain but are receiving a much-needed overhaul, keeping all of the fun but less of the cheese. Rarely for a B&B they also have two gardens, with waterfalls, and Mediterranean and Japanese themes. These are tranquil, and surprisingly private spots - if you don't count the legions of gulls poised on every surrounding roof.

Offering *"five star accommodation without the star,"* this hotel provides luxury at B&B rates. The quality extends to the breakfasts too, with a broad choice from full English, to veggie, vegan and gluten-free options.

Guest and the City
2 Broad Street, Kemp Town
(01273) 698289
Doubles £60-£140
www.guestandthecity.co.uk

Now an established example of the new breed of guesthouse with the winning formula of friendliness, beautiful modern design and proximity to the beach, and consistently rave reviews online prove its success. As with all guesthouses, everybody prefers the sea view rooms here and who can blame them? We'd encourage whatever dirty tactics you can muster (blackmail, slander, stink bombs through the letterbox) to bag one, as the superior doubles at the

front come with their own balcony and stunning stained-glass window featuring classic Brighton landmarks.

The open kitchen downstairs offers the chance for a much less formal breakfast experience (no hushed conversations and awkward rustling of newspapers), not least because of the genial owners. Thumbs up all round.

Cavalaire Hotel
34 Upper Rock Gardens, Kemptown
(01273) 696899
Singles from £75-120,
double/twin rooms from £95 to £250
www.brighton.cavalaire.co.uk

The Cavalaire has won a healthy smattering of awards, including an introduction to Tripadvisor's 'Hall of Fame', and is one of Brighton's premium B&Bs. All the rooms are lavishly decorated, with large comfy beds and en suite shower rooms with luxury toiletries provided. Owners Derek and Garry ensure a friendly service, from a glass of wine on arrival to personal recommendations for your stay in the city. The extensive breakfast menu is award-winning too - and features double egg cups!

Kemp Townhouse
21 Atlingworth Street, Kemptown
(01273) 681400
Doubles £95-215
www.kemptownhouse.com

Kemp Townhouse favours a simple elegant style, matched by a soothing conviviality. You'll find no frilly curtains or flowery duvets here, rather an elegant masculine aesthetic with a hint of Art Deco and a nod toward the seaside location with monochrome photos of sailboats. There are some particularly nice touches that demonstrate how much care has

gone into the design: the sharp red wardrobe interior, based on the lining of a Savile Row suit; and the movement triggered indigo bathroom light for avoiding waking loved ones should you need to indulge in a spot of late-night micturation. The wet room set-up in the en suites is somewhat controversial, and won't be to everyone's taste, but is a necessary compromise in a townhouse of this size. This is more than made up for in small luxuries like the range of hard and soft duck feather pillows, or the decanters of port left in each room. And you might want to stay an extra night just to sample everything on the expansive breakfast menu from the full English to the eggs Benedict.

27
27 Upper Rock Gardens, Kemp Town
(01273) 694 951
Singles from £61, doubles from £84
www.brighton-bed-and-breakfast.co.uk

Basil the peacock stands guard outside this charming B&B, and can also be found as a running motif throughout the oriental décor. 27 was recently purchased by Martin and Craig, the latter being an antiques collector and interior designer. Consequently the whole place is gorgeously done up, with antique furniture, Chinese vases and silverware creating a Pavilion-inspired atmosphere. Each of the five rooms is named for some connection to the palace, the two king doubles being the Prince Regent and Caroline of Brunswick. Try to snag one of these, as they're the only rooms with full en suites; the others have shower rooms and separate toilets.

There are nice touches like sherry in the rooms, and weather forecast cards left by your door each morning (also featuring Basil).

Myhotel

17 Jubilee Street (01273) 900300
Singles start from £90, doubles from
£110-170, penthouse from £350,
cooked breakfast £18
www.myhotels.com

As twenty-first century as Gerry
Anderson, myokcomputerhotel is
something of a love-it-or-hate-it
proposition, so singular is the vision
behind it. Describing their ethos as
Freddie Mercury meets Maharishi
Mahesh Yogi (does it get any more
Brighton?) the hotel is indeed as much
rock'n'roll as it is hippie chic. Feng
shui governs the design, with curved
furniture and walls, and healing crystals
in small alcoves in each room.

The rooms themselves are
extraordinary: floor-to-ceiling windows,
luxurious window seats and fittings
in white with splashes of neon which
conjure a Stanley Kubrick vision of the
future. Privacy advocates might find
themselves wondering if anyone can
see in from the offices opposite (we'd
suggest angling for a view of Brighton's
lovely new library instead). In fact it's
probably best that you're fairly intimate
with your room mate as well since the
bathroom doesn't have a door and
only a frosted glass panel separates
you from an encounter with their
previous night's curry. Their ridiculously
popular cocktail bar is in line with all
this uncompromising modernity but
fortunately (or disappointingly?) the
hotel staff are not robots from the
future and couldn't be friendlier. They'll
even give you a little connector to link
your iPhone to your room's invisible
surround sound system.

VERY BOHEMIAN

Blanch House
17 Atlingworth Street, Kemp Town
(01273) 603504
Rooms £105-225, breakfast included
www.blanchhouse.co.uk

Blanch House probably just pips it for being the best of the old breed of fashionable themed Brighton hotels. All twelve of the rooms are imaginative and spotless, from the beautiful Art Deco Legacia room to the smaller Alice Room with silver-embossed wallpaper, chandelier and queen-size bed. The Snowstorm room even houses a collection of snow globes to play with, and every room comes complete with DVD and flat-screen TV, chocolates and other special treats that we promised not to mention. Toss in their lovely breakfast room and bar serving specialist cocktails and you might even decide to get married here – they're licensed for it thanks to the former owners, who decided that what they really wanted to do was get married at home.

The Neo
19 Oriental Place (01273) 711104
Singles £55-65, doubles £100-160
www.neohotel.com

Maybe owner Steph is a little short-sighted, thought it was Oriental *Palace* she was moving into and decided to take up the challenge to turn her new hotel into somewhere to rival the Pavilion. Not that Neo is all dragon motifs and koi carp; the Eastern theme is largely confined to the bedrooms, which are lavishly decorated with oriental wallpaper and artwork and come with complimentary kimonos, while the king-sized chiropractor-endorsed beds and red velvet elicit thoughts of boudoir seduction. Elsewhere the hotel is decorated with objets d'art, huge chandeliers, ornate mirrors and a giant stag's head by the entrance that adds a touch of eccentricity. And Steph clearly has a love of all things black: it's a colour that prevails throughout, from the bathroom tiles to the carpets (which, yes, they hoover every day!) adding a surprisingly sumptuous feel to the place. Even the little cocktail bar – serving toffee-apple martinis – and their breakfast menus are something out of the ordinary. Stylish without being gimmicky, Neo is a rarity in Brighton: a perfect mix of glamour, eccentricity *and* elegance.

Highly recommended.

Hotel Pelirocco
10 Regency Square (01273) 327055
Singles £59-75, doubles £99-185,
suite £249-349
www.hotelpelirocco.co.uk

Undoubtedly the most outrageous of Brighton's themed hotels. There are nineteen individually themed rooms, and each one is meticulously designed down to the smallest detail, from Modrophenia, with its anorak bedspread, to 'Do Knit Disturb' (created by artist Kate Cardigan) with its knitted seagulls .

Here artistic heroes, record labels, trendy boutiques, vodka and lingerie brands have transformed each space into an individual pocket of creativity. And with such fabulous, flamboyant and unique rooms as the *Star Wars*-inspired Lord Vader's Quarters - complete with lightsaber - it is easy to see why the Pelirocco continues to attract both media attention and celebrity clientele. The crowning glory is their flagship suite, complete with eight-foot circular bed and plunge bath. This suite currently has a Kraken-hunter theme, so the mirror above the bed is advertised as a protective measure against approaching enemies. Pelirocco also has an extensive room service-style menu of erotic hampers, from the gentle 'Like A Virgin' to the more extreme 'Slave To Love'.

Snooze

25 St George's Terrace, Kemptown
(01273) 605797
Doubles £90-140, suites £110-165
www.snoozebrighton.com

This guesthouse has been decorated with both thought and zeal, from the colourful dining area to its six retro-themed doubles. These aren't exactly subtle: one's bright orange and blue with a Bollywood theme, and there's a mustard-yellow 70s room with floral wallpaper and duck wall plaques. Somehow it **works** though, through a combination of style and the clever selection of unique pieces like an eyesight test bed lamp. There are also two penthouse suites, covered in leopard and zebra print, which come with breakfast in bed.

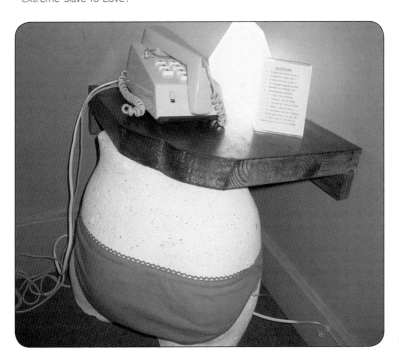

NICE & EASY DOES IT

Artist Residence

33 Regency Square (01273) 324302
Singles from £40, doubles £50-80,
breakfast not available
www.artistresidence.co.uk

There's more than a hint of Haight-Ashbury circa 1967 in the feel and rainbow-width homemade decor splashed about this quirky little hotel, but the local artists they've unleashed on the rooms haven't been allowed into the extremely modern en suites so you can always pop in there if your eyes need a rest or, if you've got a room at the front, enjoy the view of what sea is still visible behind the i360 instead. Friendly, clean and brilliant value.

Brighton House

52 Regency Square (01273) 323282
Singles £55-98, doubles £95-137,
superior doubles £114-165
www.brightonhousehotel.co.uk

This B&B has dispensed with the traditional English fry-up on grounds of health and taste and gone for an all-organic breakfast buffet which, together with stylish décor and use of environmentally-friendly cleaning products has garnered it a loyal clientele. Mr Watts, the 21-year old hotel cat, is also a big draw for returning customers, and is a cat-away-from-home for many. Brighton House's dedication to sustainability has also grabbed an extraordinary fistful of awards. Next year they're building an extension to the hotel to house them all.

Nineteen

19 Broad Street, Kemptown
(01273) 675529
Doubles from £100
www.nineteenbrighton.com

You'd be forgiven for thinking you'd entered an exclusive art gallery on walking into Nineteen. The white walls display owner Mark's eclectic contemporary collection, a colourful mix of photography, paintings and sculptures. This is just one of many features which make Nineteen refreshingly different. As Mark himself puts it, he's a *"fussy bastard"* and couldn't bear to offer people those *"horrible little plastic milks."* Instead guests can help themselves to proper coffee, hot chocolate and over twenty varieties of tea from the downstairs kitchen. Each room does have bottled South Downs mineral water and fresh fruit, and earplugs for times of heightened seagull activity.

Each of the seven bedrooms is beautiful, and has been recently refurbished with double glazing, dark oak flooring and new en suites. Room number 8 even has its own private Japanese courtyard, decorated with maples and stones from Asian riverbeds, and complete with an authentic wooden bath. Breakfast is delivered to rooms at weekends, and the menu is a healthy mix of fruit, cereals, and pastries.

Dear Customer,

Unfortunately, we have temporarily closed and sealed this Post-box due to a birds nest being present inside.

Once the eggs have hatched, we will re-open the Postbox and recommence collections on a daily basis.

An alternative posting facility is available at:
Orford Post Office, Pump Street, Orford
Post-box number: IP13 6321
M – F: 3.45pm   Sat: 11.30am

If you have any concerns you should contact our Customer Services Team on 03457 740740.

GUESTHOUSE STRIPS

If you don't have any luck with the ones listed, or fancy going it alone, you will find countless B&Bs and guesthouses in the places below. In the most traditional B&B areas, like Madeira Place, prices change daily and sometimes in accordance with what they think you'll pay, so be terribly polite and dress down for the occasion and you'll get a better offer.

Madeira Place, Lower Rock Gardens and New Steine

Close to the seafront but lacking a proper sea view. Fairly cheap, plentiful and near just about everything.

Grand Parade

Right in the town centre, ten minutes' walk from the sea and close to North Laine.

Regency Square and Bedford Square

These squares are found just past the West Pier and rooms overlook the sea (unless of course you get one at the back with a view of the gasworks).

OTHERS

For cheaper or mid-price B&Bs/hotels, here are a few that don't smell of cat wee:

Alvia Hotel
36 Upper Rock Gardens (01273) 682939

Ambassador
22 New Steine (01273) 676869

Brightonwave
10 Madeira Place (01273) 676794

Funchal Guesthouse
17 Madeira Place (01273) 603975

Keehans
57 Regency Square (01273) 327879

Leona House
74 Middle Street (01273) 327309

The LimeHouse
19 New Steine Mews (01273) 818700

The Oriental
9 Oriental Place (01273) 205050

Whitburn Lodge
12 Montpelier Road (01273) 729005

"I told you when we booked that this place looked like a right shithole."

HOSTELS

Grapevine

75-76 Middle Street & 29-30 North Road
(01273) 777717
Between £7.99 and £35 per person
www.grapevinewebsite.co.uk

What used to be Brighton
Backpackers on Middle Street had,
according to its manager, become *"a
right shithole"* but a makeover a few
years ago has meant that what is now
Grapevine Central offers, in theory,
serviceable rooms to share with up
to three other people - though it
was described by a recent guest as a
"claustrophobic, weed-smelling cave."
Not to mention that sleep might
be challenging given the number of
nightclubs opposite. There are some
en-suite doubles on the seafront side
which are a bit quieter but to be
honest there're much better hostels
available for the same money. The
North Laine version in is now the
hostel proper and is probably a better
bet for a decent snooze.

Kipps Hostel

76 Grand Parade (01273) 604182
Between £15 and £48 per person
www.kipps-brighton.com

Kipps tries to be much more like a
small hotel or B&B than a hostel - or
at least more than a place just to
dump your bags. Free events each
evening get all the guests together, and
allow solo travellers to make friends.
These often centre around food, but
also extend to Friday night cocktails,
movie nights and pub crawls. The
communal areas are homey and have
handy features: computers, Xbox, Wii,
Sky TV in the lounge area, and free tea,
coffee and cake at the bar.

The rooms are clean and you're
provided with bed linen and towels.
There are two ten-bed dorms with
lockers, and private rooms that
come with a TV, a fridge and
continental breakfast.

YHA

Old Steine, right by the Palace Pier
0845 371 9176
Beds from £15, private rooms from £35
www.yha.org.uk/hostel/brighton

Brighton's YHA is in a gorgeous building; it was originally built in 1771 and was a hotel for much of its life, most recently the Royal York as you can see in the fancy glass portico over the front entrance. The whole third floor remains as it was when a hotel, offering single and double (premium with sea view) rooms with full en suites. The other floors have a range of four, six or eight-person dorms, featuring attractive budgie-print wallpaper.

Guests have a choice between the extremely clean self-catering kitchen, and continental/full English at the breakfast bar. There's a café-restaurant, which is also the cheapest bar in Brighton (according to manager Natalie, anyway). The only downside to this hostel is noise—it's wedged between the bus station and a busy road, and often hosts school groups.

Airbnb

Prices from £18 to £1780 a night
www.airbnb.co.uk

Despite the qualms of the hotel industry which has to compete while laden down with the cost of complying with boring old legislation, this 'new economy' web service has taken off like a rocket. The system hinges on guests leaving reviews and ratings, which should allow you to be confident that your host isn't a torture fetishist. Unless their previous victims really enjoyed it.

In Brighton alone there are thousands of listed properties. Rent a bed from a woman and her *"loveable cats."* Enjoy the sea views from a luxury Kemptown penthouse. Spend a week in an Alice in Wonderland-themed Regency home. You can even spend the weekend in a moated castle, enjoying the services of a butler, maid and cook, and conversation with its predictably eccentric owner, Quentin.

CAMPING

Brighton Caravan Club

Behind the Marina off Wilson Avenue
(01273) 626546
www.caravanclub.co.uk

Non-member peak charges – caravan from £25-£40ish a night with electric hook-up, two people in a tent (with car parking) starts at £20 ish per night.

Pop-up Camping

Bevendean Farm, Warren Avenue
07771 535350
Open from May-September (Fri-Sun only)
popupcampsites.com/pop-up-in-brighton

This campsite is in a beautiful location on the South Downs but still relatively close to the city. You can pitch your own tent for £12.50 per person per night, or treat yourself to some *glamping* (ugh) in one of the bell tents at £100 for the weekend. or go all the way to £300 for a pre-constructed tent, ready for your arrival with all the sheepskin rugs and fairy lights that any Antarctic camping expedition would be lost without. Add £25 for a power point to charge your phone, £7 for breakfast in bed, and the on-site holistic therapist and you should be able to forget you're camping at all.

The facilities are clean and include hot showers and pamper tables. You could also be a bit daring and use one of the eco composting toilets, or the gas-powered showers which have beautiful views over the downs. The daily 'bushcraft' lessons are ideal for families and include fire-making, axe-throwing, spoon carving, and donkey smacking.

Outside Brighton

Beachy Head

This notorious suicide spot features in the closing scenes of *Quadrophenia* and gets a mention in several Monty Python sketches. It is also a popular spot for birders as plenty of migrant oddities that get blown over the water stop here to catch their breath and visit the 24-hour All You Can Eat Worm Café. It can get pretty windy up here so be careful near the edge but do look out for the red-and-white striped lighthouse and the spooky old burned-out car halfway down the cliffs. It takes about 45 minutes to reach Beachy Head from Brighton but it s worth the visit for the spectacular views and having the proverbial cobwebs blown away. There s also a pub nearby if you get thirsty, though the Samaritans adverts can be a sobering reminder of the area's legacy.

Chanctonbury Ring
5 miles north of Worthing

This small Iron-Age hill fort, noted for its ring of beech trees (though most, sadly, were lost in the hurricane of 1987) is a beguiling place steeped in folklore. According to legend, if you walk or run seven times around the Ring at midnight, the devil will appear, offering a bowl of milk, soup or porridge. If you accept these comestibles, he'll take your soul or offer you your heart's desire. Legend has it this is how Noel Edmonds got back on telly with *Deal or No Deal*.

Chanctonbury Ring is also associated with sighting of UFOs and fairies; there have been countless reports over the years of strange coloured objects and dancing lights. Even nature writer Robert MacFarlane describes a sense of terror when visiting here, in his book *The Old Ways*. If you're planning a visit, it's best not to come alone. And certainly not at night.

Devil's Dyke

So the story goes that the devil started to dig a deep chasm to let the sea in to drown all the pious villagers of the Weald. But an old lady – on hearing the sound of the devil's mechanical digger – lit a candle in her window, held it in front of a colander and tricked him into believing it was sunrise. The devil scarpered but his unfinished business – a 300-foot valley in the heart of the South Downs – remained.

Now there are several flaws in this local myth – like what kind of idiot mistakes a colander and candle for the sunrise, and why didn't the devil just come back the following night anyway? – but we'll let it pass as it's a good yarn.

A visit to the Dyke is heartily recommended; this striking geographical feature offers plenty of opportunity for long walks, terrific views across the Downs and a shortcut down the steep hill to the Shepherd & Dog in Fulking for steak-and-ale pie, chips, a few pints and a heart attack as you attempt the journey back. The Dyke is a fifteen-minute drive out of Brighton and in summer you can even catch an open-top bus there from the city centre. Be prepared for crowds at the weekend and (allegedly) dogging in the car park at night.

Ditchling

A quintessential English village with a few famous inhabitants, good pubs and a cake shop with the best treacle tart in the world. Past the strange little museum and village pond as the road bends to the left there's a stile and a very agreeable walk offering excellent views of the Downs. Go up the hill, take a picnic, enjoy the view and expect to share your field with a few friendly cows. Alternatively, park at the village hall, take a right and follow signposts up to the Downs.

Cheeky fact: an amateur production of Alice Through the Looking Glass, performed at Ditchling Village Hall in 1969 starred an eight year old Martha Kearney (now of Radio 4 fame). The original album of songs recorded from this production, and credited to Peter Howell, is now one of the most sought-after psych-folk albums in the world.

Eastbourne

To some Brightonians, Eastbourne is the world s largest open-plan hospice, offering more hearing-aid shops than

cafés, a neat line in poodle parlours and a population of the walking dead. And while this isn't too far from the truth (OK it is the truth), this sedentary coastal town still has enough tricks up its sleeve to merit a visit, even if you *are* under 60. As well as the very pretty area known as the Old Town (for obvious reasons), Eastbourne has a surprisingly attractive seafront. Lacking the naff commercialism of Brighton's front, Eastbourne's is – rather refreshingly – adorned with lush greenery. In summer the promenade teems with palm trees, flowerbeds, bushes and trees, brass bands are in full swing and old couples in cardies and blazers stroll along arm in arm. Add to this the facts that the beach is far cleaner than Brighton's, the pebbles are smaller and the pier and seafront aren't rammed with drunk Londoners and hen parties, and the prospect of spending a lazy day here sloping around, lounging on the beach and swimming can be very appealing.

Of course one shouldn't get too carried away. Eastbourne's town centre could rival that of Swindon's for grimness, but when the grime and chaos of Brighton get too much for you, a day out here *can* feel like a nice long soak in the bath. Just don't stay too long – you might end up all wrinkly.

Lewes

On the surface Lewes is a cosy little town, ideal for taking your parents to for an afternoon stroll round the castle, shopping for distressed furniture and jam, a swim at the outdoor Pells Pool and a pint of Harvey's. Below the surface of town however, beats a dark pagan heart; Lewes is host to the largest fireworks event in the UK (see *What's On* chapter), which is the closest you'll ever get to feeling like you've stepped into the final scene of *The Wicker Man*.

There are some wonderful pubs here, notably the Lewes Arms, tucked away down one of the many side streets. It has been host to a number of bizarre games including 'Toads' and an annual Pea Throwing Competition (the rules of which are very amusing). It's probably your best port of call for a real taste of Lewes and a chance to meet some of the town's fruitier characters.

Stanmer Park

Head out of Brighton for a few miles on the A27 (Lewes Road) towards Sussex University and you'll find this expansive park and woodland. There's ample room here for big footy games, frisbee throwing and a chance to take some long rambles in the woods. There's also an organic farm, a small church, lovely tea rooms and an annual Apple Day. Look out for the tree trunk carved into badgers behind Stanmer House and the pet cemetery in the woods. Extra brownie points if you find the Earthship, a startling demonstration of how much cash you could stop giving EDF and Southern Water if you built your house out of old tyres, crisp packets and mud.

Worthing and Goring
www.sistinechapeluk.co.uk

Those who find the pace of life in Eastbourne too soporific will doubtless find Worthing catatonic, bringing to mind the lyrics of the old Morrissey song *Everyday is Like Sunday* (sic). This once-popular seaside resort has barely changed in 50 years but therein lies its (limited) appeal. When you've spent enough time in Brighton to grow a little weary of every day being like Saturday, a day trip to a faded, sleepy seaside town can be a refreshing reminder of a gentler pace of life.

Visit Worthing on a warm summer's day (any other time would be foolhardy) and you can enjoy a stroll along a seafront that time forgot: a movie at the old Art Deco cinema, the old pier with many amusement games still only 2p (including the charming Monkey Band at the back that kids will love despite the drummer having apparently died), a coffee at Coast, the open-air hexagonal café five minutes from the pier, or liver and bacon at the fantastic 50s caféteria opposite (frequented by Harold Pinter when he lived here in the 60s).

If you need a few oohs and aaaahs prompted by local landmarks, seek out the Martyrs Church in Goring where a local artist has lovingly (and painstakingly) recreated the ceiling of the Sistine Chapel. Or head up to Lancing College, the impressive Pratchett-esque Gothic building you can see from the A27 when travelling west; the church and crypt are open to the public, while the grounds have a commanding view of the Downs, the beach and Shoreham Airport and are a good spot for a quiet picnic.

Forget good shopping, nightlife and excitement in Worthing: they barely exist, but for a spot of irony-free retro and a bit of peace and quiet as once found here by Oscar Wilde (hence Mr Worthing in *The Importance of Being Earnest*), an afternoon in Worthing in the summer can be a tonic for the nerves.

BRIGHTON PEERS
by Cool CHEESE

TRAFFIC WARDEN

LIVES:- NEAR WITHDEAN WHERE SHE USES THE 'PARK AND RIDE' SCHEME TO GET INTO WORK

SPOTTED:- PATROLLING YOUR STREET EVERY FOUR HOURS, SEVEN DAYS A WEEK

"MOVE IT!" LOOK ON FACE

ANGRY MOTORIST'S WAVING FINGER

'BACK - UP'

EPAULETTES TO GIVE UNIFORM MILITARY SIGNIFICANCE

ENORMOUS WALKIE TALKIE FOR TIP-OFFS FROM COLLEAGUES IN THE NEXT STREET

ELECTRONIC NOTEBOOK WHICH CAN PRINT UP TO 1,000 TICKETS PER HOUR

WITH ALL THAT **WALKING** THEY DO, WHY DO **TRAFFIC WARDENS** ALWAYS LOOK SO **UNFIT**?

Useful Info

ARRIVING BY RAIL

National Rail Enquiries
03457 48 49 50
www.nationalrail.co.uk
www.southernrailway.com

Trains from London leave Victoria and Kings Cross Thameslink about twice an hour. The Victoria link is usually quicker – about 50 minutes for the fast train. Be careful when returning to London late at night however, if you miss the last train around midnight you'll have hours to wait for the next one. There are also direct train services along the coast if you are not coming via London.

Sunday trains

Irritatingly, National Rail (or whoever) have been 'repairing' the line between Brighton and London now for more than 300 years. Why it is taking them so long to fix 40-odd miles of track is a mystery but it does mean that if you catch the London-to-Brighton train on a Sunday your journey could take several hours as you find yourself rerouted via Littlehampton, Eastbourne and Barnsley, shoved onto a bus for half your journey and then fined £50 on arrival for your ticket being an Awaydaysupersaver instead of a Superdayawaysaver. We kid you not, we have spent some miserable Sunday evenings dreaming of being at home by the fire sipping fine wines, when instead we're standing in the rain in the middle of sodding nowhere, waiting for some surly driver who turns up an hour late and doesn't seem to know where he's going. And to top it all, after five minutes the bloody bus breaks down. And there're no free seats. And yes, this has happened more times than we care to mention. Now that's off our chests we feel much better. Ignore this at your peril!

ARRIVING BY PLANE

From Gatwick

A train will get you to Brighton in twenty minutes. If there are four of you a taxi may actually cost less. The cheapest option is to get a coach or walk.

From Heathrow

It's a drag, to be honest. The simplest option is a coach that'll go via every Heathrow terminal and Gatwick and take about three hours. Otherwise it's tubes and trains via London, which is quicker but a pain if you've got heavy cases.

If you can persuade someone to collect you from/take you to Heathrow and you're both single, the least you can do is ask them to marry you.

ARRIVING BY COACH

National Express
08717 818181
www.nationalexpress.com

While they do take twice as long as the train and often reek of chemical loos, if you're flying in or out of Gatwick in the small hours (courtesy of a cheapo EasyJet flight) this is a better bet than a £50 cab fare.

ARRIVING BY CAR

Once you've packed your sandwiches, toothbrush, bucket and spade, make your way to the London orbital then take the M23/A23 all the way to Brighton. It shouldn't take more than 45 minutes once you've left the M25. It's as simple as that. To avoid the horrendous traffic jams it's best to stay off the M25 any time between 7am and midnight. If you're lucky enough not to be coming via London you'll probably be taking the coastal route along the A27. To avoid the horrendous traffic jams there, it's best to stay off between 7am and midnight.

ARRIVING BY HELICOPTER

You'll get as far as Shoreham Airport and then it's a two-hour walk to Brighton along the seafront. What do you mean you haven't got a helicopter?

BUSES

Brighton & Hove Bus Company
(01273) 886200
www.buses.co.uk

The Big Lemon
(01273) 681681
www.thebiglemon.com

Buses in Brighton are frequent and plentiful. So plentiful in fact that Western Road is chockablock with them day and night, resulting in the world's first ever bus-only gridlock which lasted for more than eighteen hours in 2015. There is a flat fare of £2.40 which only seems economical if travelling long distances like Worthing to Peacehaven, but you can now travel for £2 within the city centre and some short-hop routes like the station to the pier are £1.80.

Also worth celebrating is The Big Lemon, a local company whose buses are run entirely on used cooking oil collected from Brighton restaurants. Unfortunately they don't run all over town; their only public service is the Woodingdean to Old Steine route via the Marina - which allegedly is forced by the council to use the same fares as the main bus company - and they run a student-only free shuttle between Falmer and the city centre.

Top tip: The Big Lemon buses are available for private hire and also run a service to a lot of festivals including Glastonbury each year.

Open-Top Bus Tour
April-September, tours daily from 10.30am
www.city-sightseeing.com

Brighton for lazybones. Do the lot in one hour for £11. Meet opposite the Pool Valley coach station on Brighton seafront.

TAXIS

(01273) 202020 • 204060 • 747474 • 205205

There are plenty to choose from and all the services are pretty much the same. Only two types of Brighton taxi driver seem to exist: the friendly cabby who chats amiably all the way to your destination and the silent, morose type whose only words are "*fucking idiot*", which he shouts at every other driver on the road. Unsurprisingly, taxi fares in Brighton are among the highest in the country and more expensive per mile than flying Concorde (RIP). Taxi drivers in Brighton are required by law to carry inflatable life jackets under their seats so check when you get in. If there isn't one you should be able to blag a free ride.

CITY CAR CLUB

0845 330 1234
www.citycarclub.co.uk

A cracking idea for a town with nowhere to park (and sinking into the sea under the weight of traffic), City Car Club is a pay-as-you-go car-hire service with designated parking bays close to where you live. It's dead easy to join: go online, book it for a minimum of an hour, open the doors with a smart card, punch in your PIN number and you're off! Brrm brrm!!

BRIGHTON SUBWAY

Closed because of subsidence and waterlogging, Brighton's once-famous Metro line used to stretch as far as Eastbourne, Worthing and London. Nowadays it is notable for Brighton's expanding subterranean community, several fight clubs and occasional sightings of the Brunswick Yeti.

WALKING

Visitors from LA might be interested to learn that this mode of transport is still immensely popular in Brighton.

BIKES

Along with *The Simpsons* (series three to nine), cheese on toast and the Walkman, bikes remain one of humankind's greatest achievements. And despite the hills, Brighton is ideal for cyclists; you can be just about anywhere in under fifteen minutes (provided you smoke less than 40 a day). Unfortunately the council's botch-job cycle lanes are far from ideal. You'll be taking your life in your hands cycling along Western Road and North Street, where there aren't *any* cycle lanes and the constant

cavalcade of buses squeezes you off the road onto the busy pavement. Elsewhere – such as parts of North Laine where cyclists can go the wrong way down one-way streets – things are equally hazardous. While contraflows work in a cyclist's favour in theory, in practice drivers do not seem to respect or realise cyclists have the right of way here and will often just drive at you, forcing you off the road or worse.

To end on a more positive note, we've been cycling round Brighton for twenty years and lived to tell the tale, a lot of new high quality long distance lanes have been built in the last few years and the seafront really is great for bikes – it's long and flat and you can go all the way from Hove to the Marina and Rottingdean via the undercliff pass. In summer though, invest in a horn; you'll be spending half your time dodging the dozy gits who walk in the seafront cycle lanes.

Weird Cycle Lanes

by freewheelin' cyclin' spokes-man
Alan 'Fred' Pipes

Brighton & Hove, which in October 2005 received £3 million of government money as a Cycling Demonstration Town, has lots and lots of cycle lanes. However, they don't all join up. In fact, few do, and there are many strange short ones here and there to mystify urban cyclists, who are forever told to dismount, walk a couple of feet along wide pavements, and then remount.

These have been documented in *www.weirdcyclelanes.co.uk*, a website started in 2000 that grew out of an article in *The Guardian* claiming that some cycle lane Up North was the shortest in Britain. The shortest in Brighton at the time was by the Gloucester nightclub (now the North Laine Brewhouse) and led into North Laine, but stopped after about a car's length. As time went by, even shorter and weirder ones began appearing!

This town (er, city) has a love/hate relationship with cyclists and the letters page of *The Argus* is filled with apoplectic correspondents from Hove banging on about demon cyclists jumping red lights, going down St James's Street the wrong way, cycling on pavements and not paying 'road tax'. Hove Esplanade, in particular, although about a mile wide, is festooned with No Cycling signs and guarded by impenetrable barriers each end.

The problem is that the land for cycle lanes is either stolen from the roads, thus annoying motorists who need to park on them, or from the pavements, thus incurring the wrath of pedestrians who like nothing better than to stroll nonchalantly along the seafront cycle lanes between the piers. Should a cyclist swerve to avoid any of them, they are liable for an instant thirty-quid fine for cycling on the pavement from one of our growing number of cycle bobbies!

PARKING

Devilishly tricky *and* expensive. Parking meters and resident parking zones have been phased in for most of the city centre. There are, however, several multi-storey car parks in the town, which are all signposted.

One good wheeze if visiting for the day in spring or summer is to park in the cheapest car park - at the far end of Madeira Drive by the Marina, a quarter of the price they charge in the Lanes at weekends - and then take the Volks electric train to the Palace Pier. Alternatively and slightly less scenically, use the park and ride at Withdean (on the way into town on the A23) where the parking is free and the Saturday bus ride will cost you the equivalent of one hour in a city centre multi-storey.

Or just park illegally anywhere for more than ten minutes and get a massive fine.

A few parking facts

1. Brighton traffic wardens once issued a ticket to a hearse (the undertakers were moving a body), thus breaching the city's own parking laws.

2. All meters are solar-powered. If a piece of card is placed over the solar panel on the top of the meter, the meter ceases to function after three days. Erm, allegedly.

3. Parking tickets are issued at a rate of one every two minutes in Brighton.

4. In 2013, parking charges generated £16 million profit for Brighton Council, the highest figure outside London.

5. Traffic wardens deserve our pity and *not* our contempt, as they are victims of a loveless childhood.

An illegally parked café A-board gets its third ticket of the day

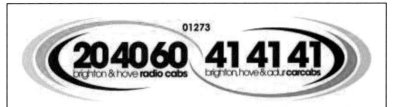

TOURIST INFORMATION

Visitor Information Contact Centre

(01273) 290337
Mon-Sat and summer Sundays 10am-4pm
www.visitbrighton.com

The old premium priced phone line has now been replaced by an ordinary local call rate number. Hooray!

Visitor Information Points

www.visitbrighton.com

No less than fourteen information points now exist across the city centre. The most useful are probably those at the train station and the pier since those are where most tourists find themselves at some stage. The most comprehensive is now to be found at the Brighton Centre box office on the seafront, where they can sort out on-the-day bookings for B&Bs and hotels, as well as National Express coaches and day trips. You'll also find all the customary gubbins about local tours, museums and places to visit.

City Champions

www.visitbrighton.com/city-champions

Back in the 1950s Brighton had a team of young women called The Promettes, who wandered around the seafront dressed like air stewardesses, offering advice and guidance to visitors. A Pathé news film of the time described them as *"walking mines of information - with sex appeal added!"* The concept has now been revived in a slightly more enlightened form with the City Champions, whose membership is no longer confined to *"trainee models who make life just one long holiday for visitors - if you know what we mean!"* Watch out for folks outfitted in blue and orange who hang around the station and the Royal Pavilion at weekends - they might look like charity muggers but all they want to do is recommend you a restaurant or direct you to your desired destination.

CRIME

As with any UK city, don't walk around with your wallet hanging out of your back pocket and you should be fine. Hang around on West Street at the weekend for long enough however and you will be robbed by junkies, stripped naked by loose women, beaten up by lager louts and pecked to death by seagulls.

LATE NIGHT EATING

Buddies

46-48 Kings Road, Brighton seafront, just down from the Odeon (01273) 323600
buddies24hour.net

The Market Diner

19-21 Circus Street (01273) 608273
marketdinerbrighton.co.uk

The Brighton Bystander

1 Terminus Road, Brighton (01273) 823322

A baby in a jar

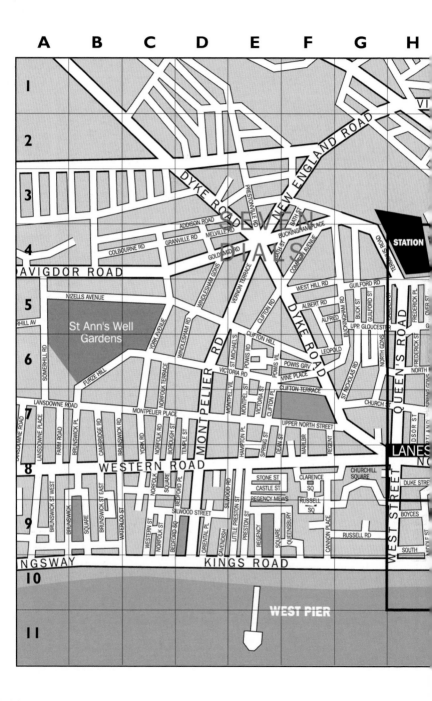

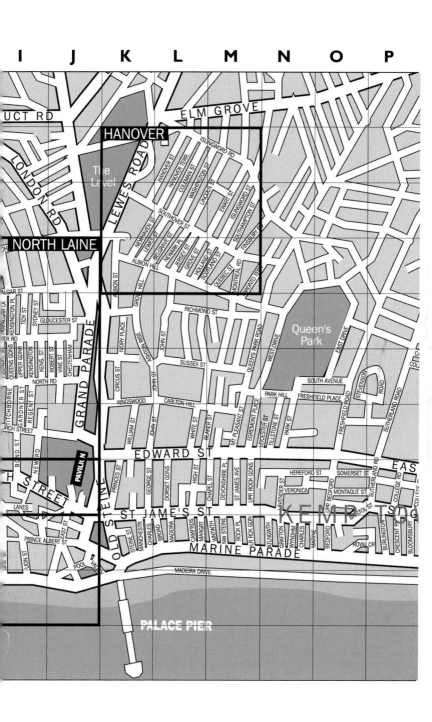

UCT RD

ELM GROVE

HANOVER

The Level

LEWES ROAD

LONDON RD

ISLINGWORD RD

HANOVER ST
HANOVER TERR
COLEMAN ST
WASHINGTON ST
LINCOLN ST
EWART ST
ISLINGWORD ST
SOUTHAMPTON ST
FINSBURY RD

SOUTHOVER ST

NORTH LAINE

NEWHAVEN ST
LEWES ST
BELGRAVE PL
NEWARK PL
JERSEY ST
GROVE ST
TOLLAND ST
SCOTLAND ST
QUEBEC ST
MONTREAL RD
TORONTO TERR

ALBION HILL

ALBION ST

GROVE HILL

RICHMOND ST

Queen's Park

WEST DRIVE

EAST DRIVE

ALGAR ST
KENSINGTON LA
KENSINGTON PL
TIDY ST
SYDNEY ST
GLOUCESTER ST

IVORY PLACE

ASHTON RISE

JOHN ST

QUEEN'S PARK ROAD

SUSSEX ST

SOUTH AVENUE

PARK HILL

FRESHFIELD PLACE

STEVENSON ROAD

SUTHERLAND ROAD

QUEENS GDNS
UPPER GDNR
KENSINGTON
KENS. ST
VINE ST
ROBERT ST
CHELTENHAM
NORTH RD

GRAND PARADE

CIRCUS ST

JOHN ST

KINGSWOOD

CARLTON HILL

TITCHBORNE
GARDNER ST
REGENT ST

WILLIAM ST

JOHN ST

WHITE ST

BLAKER ST

MT PLEASANT ST

EGREMONT PLACE

LEICESTER ST

TILLSTONE ST

PARK ST

FRESHFIELD ROAD

CHURCH STREET

EDWARD ST

EAS

BROAD ST

NEW RD

PAVILION

PRINCES ST

GEORGE ST

DORSET GDNS

HIGH ST

CHAPEL ST

DEVONSHIRE PL

ST JAMES AVE

UPP ROCK GDNS

HEREFORD ST

SOMERSET ST

SUTHERLAND RD

COLLEGE RD

LANES

OLD STEINE

ST JAMES'S ST

LAVENDER ST

VERONICA

MONTAGUE ST

BEDFORD

KEMP TO

EAST ST
PRINCE ALBERT ST

STEINE ST
MANCHESTER
CHARLES
BROAD
MADEIRA
CAMFRDS
MARGRT
WYNTH
NW STEINE
ROCK PL
LR ROCK GDN

WATLNGWTH
GRAFTON
WYNDM
CHARLES
MARINE

BRISTOL RD
BURLINGTON
CRESCENT RD
BLOOMSBURY
ROYAL CR

KEMP TOG

LION ST

POOL

VALLEY

MARINE PARADE

MADEIRA DRIVE

PALACE PIER

250

O Fishly Healthy
109 St James's Street (01273) 958260

Passionate about quality, taste experiences and cooking methods, every day we open with wonderful and varied fresh fish, exotic fish and seafood ready on the counter. All fish comes from local, sustainable sources or are managed purchases of exotic imports that avoid the callous abuse of the planet's resources.

Plateau
1 Bartholomews (01273) 733085

Natural wine bar and restaurant, the emphasis is on the raw product, quality, provenance and taste. Our wines are natural, that is organic or biodynamic as a minimum, real, vibrant, alive and expermailtly made by passionate artisans. We also serve cocktails, made by a team considered the best in town!

The Old Market
Upper Market St. Hove (01273) 201801

Hove's independent, high quality live theatre and venue holds up to 300 seated, or 500 standing. Owned and managed by the creative directors behind international smash-hit show STOMP, The Old Market's diverse programme includes live music, great theatre, innovative comedy and premium club nights. Check what's on: *theoldmarket.com*

Short & Girlie Show
www.shortandgirlie.com

Award winning all-female comedy improvisation troupe based in Brighton, London and Bristol. Shows. Workshops for all ages. Compering. Private parties. Event production. The only Brighton company to offer regular women-only workshops, providing escapism, creativity and laughter. Everyone welcome.

Planet India

(01273) 818149

Authentic home made Indian food made by authentic home made Indians

Time to relax!
07586 296 703 (Ingrid)

We are 2 fully qualified professional therapists who provide a high quality side by side massage service for couples, families or friends in the comfort of your own home. Perfect treat for birthdays, Valentines, hen parties... Choose from: Swedish, Aromatherapy, Deep tissue, Pregnancy and Indian Head Massage.

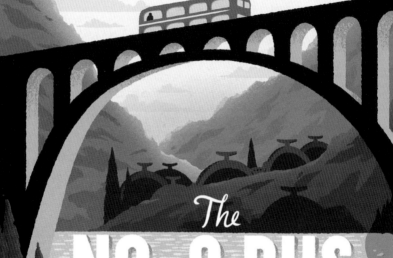

HOW ONE MAN'S EXTRAORDINARY
JOURNEY LED TO A QUIET REVOLUTION

The
NO. 9 BUS
To
UTOPIA

DAVID
BRAMWELL

Also by David Bramwell

THE No9 BUS TO UTOPIA

Packed with gags, wisdom and pathos, this actually is a must-read
Tom Hodgkinson (How to be Idle)

As compassionate as it is funny. David Bramwell has written a very
important book pretending to be otherwise.
Tim Smit (Dir. Eden Project)

A remarkable storyteller
(Radio Times)

'One of the best non-fiction books I read in 2015 (and I read a lot)
(Stevyn Colgan, QI elf)

After his girlfriend leaves him for someone she describes as 'younger, but
more mature', David sets himself a life-changing task: to be a more sharing,
loving person. As a man with a taste for the exotic however, this is never
going to be resolved by an eight week course in 'Mindfulness'. Instead,
David embarks on a global adventure to learn how to live with others.
He visits an anarchist community in the heart of Copenhagen, a futuristic
city in the desert and believes he's found paradise in a Californian retreat,
dreamt up by Aldous Huxley. Most fantastic of all is Damanhur, a thou-
sand-strong community in the Italian Alps, with an underground temple
the size of St Paul's Cathedral and a 'fully functioning time machine'.

Along the way, David's quest throws up other niggling issues that beset
many of us: Why is unhappiness rife amongst those who have wealth and
freedom? How can we re-instill community spirit in our densely populated
cities? Is getting what you want really utopian? And if alternative com-
munities hold the answer to how we should live, why do so many of their
inhabitants still insist on wearing tie-dye?

This wry, self-deprecatingly funny and philosophical book asks some big
questions and finds the answers surprisingly simple.

drbramwell.com

What people are saying about Tim Bick

"Excellent"
(Simon Raymonde, Bella Union/Cocteau Twins)

"Britpop without the cockney accent"
(Kevin Wright, The Sound Of Confusion)

"We're big fans"
(Tom Robinson)

"Behind the dry-wit lyrics and quirky vocal approach is a well put together tune that boasts an unfussy and really likeably catchy main melody"
(Andy Leigh, Chartburst.com)

"I have literally never heard of him"
(Tony Visconti, producer)

"I love his music, but when he started his musician's advice show The Music Muddle (it's available at **www.youtube.com/MrTimBick** apparently) I thought it was taking the piss a bit, I mean, that's my job isn't it, giving guidance and stuff? Most of what he says in the show is basically lies."
(Shel Valentine, Tim's manager)

www.starstarstarstar.com

Also by Tim Bick

Also available...

CHEEKY WALKS

IN BRIGHTON & SUSSEX

A WALK BOOK LIKE NO OTHER!

A UNIQUE THEME FOR EVERY WALK -

ART, LORD LUCAN, SEX, DEATH, FOOTBALL, KATIE PRICE, TWITTENS, PLAQUES, NIGHT WALKING, A MUSICAL SOUNDTRACK....

www.cheekyguides.com